Wisconsin Waterfalls

1-23-99

Herman

Please enjoy this
waterfall book
and
Wisconsin Natural Resources

Patrick J. Lisi

Wisconsin Waterfalls

A Touring Guide

Patrick J. Lisi

Prairie Oak
P R E S S

Madison, Wisconsin

First edition, first printing
Copyright © 1998 by Patrick J. Lisi

Prairie Oak Press
821 Prospect Place
Madison, WI 53703

Designed and produced by Flying Fish Graphics, Blue Mounds, Wisconsin
Printed in Korea

All photographs by the author
Front cover photo: *Copper Falls, Bad River*
Back cover photo: *Potato River Falls*

Library of Congress Cataloging-in-Publication Data

Lisi, Patrick J.
      Wisconsin waterfalls : a touring guide/ by Patrick Lisi
      —1st ed.
           p. cm.
      ISBN 1-879483-50-5 (alk. paper)
1. Waterfalls—Wisconsin—Guidebooks. 2. Waterfalls–Wisconsin—Pictorial works. I. Title.
GB1425.W6L58 1998
551.48'4'09775—dc21   98-8215
                                                        CIP

To Marjorie
Who changed my life

Contents

ACKNOWLEDGMENTS

A project of this magnitude is successful because of the effort and assistance of many people. I would like to thank all the marvelous people throughout Wisconsin who wrote to me with suggestions and locations of waterfalls near their homes. I wanted to include as many waterfalls as possible in this book and I was very grateful when folks pointed out their favorite cascades.

I extend my deepest gratitude to Jerry Minnich, president of Prairie Oak Press, who showed undying faith in us and our project and the encouragement to keep it on track. And to Kristin Visser, Caroline Beckett, and Frank Sandner, who edited and designed the book you hold in your hand.

Our thanks to son Tom Lisi for his detailed work on how to calculate the flow of water over a waterfall, which you will find in Chapter 10.

Thanks also to Eric Glindinning, who lives just east of Pattison State Park in Douglas County, and who was kind enough to guide Marjorie and me to Copper Creek Falls one sunny, spring afternoon.

Special thanks to Steve and Julie Sorensen, owners of the Northward Bookstore, 410 W. Lake Shore Drive, Ashland, for their assistance in procuring the topographical maps used to pinpoint the waterfalls in the book.

A special "thank you" to Bill Smith, Washburn chiropractor and friend, for his work on Minnehaha Falls, and to Miss Dempsey, my childhood friend who first told me about the glorious waterfalls of northern Wisconsin.

Finally, and most importantly, I acknowledge the supreme handiwork of Almighty God who created all of the glorious wonders of nature that we on Earth have the privilege to behold, including the fantastic waterfalls featured in this book.

FOREWORD

In 1991 the quest began. It was born partly out of desire for quiet adventure and solitude, but mostly from my terrific curiosity about the geology of Wisconsin and how the state was shaped by the forces of nature. I wanted to learn about Wisconsin's rivers, their headwaters, their routes, and how many waterfalls decorate Wisconsin's rivers. I soon found myself involved in an undertaking that consumed me; all my free time was spent afield, cameras and notebook in hand, sometimes alone and often times accompanied by one of my sons, Tom or Tim. Anytime I got wind of a waterfall that I hadn't previously known about, I was off to explore.

I am continually attracted to waterfalls for many reasons. Each one stimulates my senses in a slightly different way and with varying intensity. Every waterfall has a character and a personality of its own, and it is never boring to repeatedly visit the same waterfall, because they are constantly in motion and subject to change at a moment's notice. High water in the spring might bring logs that become snagged in the crown of a waterfall. Summer means less water flow in the river and is a perfect time to view the layers of bedrock at the falls and to examine its geological composition. In autumn brightly colored leaves gently drift down the river and then abruptly disappear down the face of the waterfall, and winter is a season when the serious adventurer straps on snowshoes for a walk to a favorite cascade.

As you explore the magnificent waterfalls of Wisconsin and the upper Midwest, do not rush to see them all. Spend time relaxing and contemplating as you sit on the rocks or a fallen tree along the riverbank. Try to imagine where all that rushing water is coming from and follow the stream in your mind's eye to its final destination. Look closely at the waterfall and try to feel the energy and the raw power of this awesome creation. Ponder the surge you would feel in your body if you were a few gallons of water flying out over the crest of the falls, swan-diving into the pool below. Think of how graceful and soft the waterfall really is, and then realize its destructive capacity and how it has scoured and etched the stony slab beneath it for tens of thousands of years. Ponder the river as it relates to the life of the landscape around it, and see the waterfall as a moment in time.

When you venture into the woods and hike along the rivers in search of the waterfalls in this book, remember there are many other waterfalls in Wisconsin. In fact, when you reach a portion of a river that has the geological conditions for one waterfall, you can assume there is probably another one close by, up or downstream. It is fun to explore other stretches of the river looking for these hidden cascades. Amnicon Falls State Park, for example, has no less than seven splendid waterfalls!

Waterfall hunting is a wonderful family activity. It is quiet, peaceful, and a perfect way to spend time outdoors with people you love. Our family has grown closer over the years as we shared the fun of searching out waterfalls throughout the United States. Mother Nature can do the same for you.

Map Symbols

Dam site	
View of the falls from the road	
Handicap accessible	
Campsites	
Fishing	
Cross-country skiing	X
Picnic tables	
Toilet facilities	
Hiking Trails-	
Easy	E
Moderate	M
Strenuous	S

(Preceding page) *Big Manitou Falls, Pattison State Park*   (above) *Lake Superior shoreline*

Chapter 1
DOUGLAS AND BAYFIELD COUNTIES

It was a nippy, breezy, and exhilarating mid-afternoon late in September at Pattison State Park. The forest surrounding me was ablaze with colorful reds, oranges, and yellows as maples, birches, and oaks showed off their colors as winter approached the southwest basin of Lake Superior. Interspersed in the bright colors, green spires of conifers jutted through the canopy. I relaxed on the moist but warm sand on the shore below Big Manitou Falls, my legs folded under me. The relentless pounding crashed through me like the roar of a freight train as I peered at the lip of the waterfall 165 feet above.

Spray glazed my face and I savored the chill that pierced my skin. I soon became used to the temperature of the water. Every now and then the sun would peek from behind a fluffy cloud and warm me with a momentary ray.

Though hidden from view, the approach and the lip of Big Manitou was clear in my mind—a deep, brackish pool in the Black River where hundreds of thousands of gallons of water eddied before funneling through the narrows at the crown of the waterfall, then down over jagged rock and boulders. Mesmerized by the flow of water before me, I lost track of time. The sun had gone down behind a stand of spruce to the southwest and I was in shadow. The moisture in the already cool air brought me to my senses, and I realized I was soaked from head to toe, and that the day was coming to an end.

As I stood up and stretched, an immature bald eagle soared up the Black River, emitting a single shrill call, up and over Big Manitou, and then out of sight. I smiled as I watched the graceful predator disappear into the bluish-gray haze. I plucked my camera bag from the ground and headed for the trail.

Big Manitou Falls, Black River

Little Manitou Falls, Black River

DOUGLAS COUNTY
Big Manitou Falls
Little Manitou Falls
Copper Creek Falls

Location: Black River, 13 miles south of Superior, Pattison State Park.

At 165 feet, Big Manitou is a giant among waterfalls. It is the fourth highest waterfall east of the Rocky Mountains within the continental United States, and it towers over all other waterfalls in Wisconsin. Big Manitou is the premier feature at Pattison State Park, an impeccably kept camping and hiking paradise nestled among stately conifer and hardwood forests along a ridge of rolling hills 15 miles from the southwest shore of Lake Superior.

Twelve thousand years ago the glacier that covered this area began to melt. The melting waters helped form Lake Superior. They also formed rivers as they cut through the glacial sediment and began to erode the billion-year-old volcanic basalt rock that was beneath the sediments. These volcanic rocks are evident in the bed of the Black River as it flows through the park. Today's landscape is the result of flowing water eroding the glacial sediments and the softest of the ancient volcanic rocks.

There are vistas on both the north and south rims of the 165-foot cliff at the head of Big Manitou Falls. From the north vista you can see the waterfall plunge into the pool at the bottom and watch the foamy eddies and swirls before the water gushes downstream on its way to Lake Superior. From three viewing areas on the south rim you can see all of Big Manitou (this is the best location for photos) and the river at the base of the falls as it swirls around a rock outcropping and then shoots down the watery tube into the main stream. The falls can be heard from just about anywhere on the west side of Hwy 35 within the park.

A short trail leads to the northern vista, which is protected by railings, of course, and a longer trail takes you to the vistas on the south side, also guarded by railings and fieldstone barriers along the stone and cement stairway leading to the viewing areas.

This 1,373-acre park is named for lumber baron Martin Pattison of Superior, who had the foresight to preserve both Big Manitou Falls and Little Manitou Falls by purchasing the initial 660 acres and donating the land to the state. Pattison State Park was developed in 1920.

Little Manitou Falls abruptly drop 31 feet from

Copper Creek Falls

a deep pool that is amazingly still and peaceful, bounding into the black basin below. At the base of the falls the water is calm again.

You can follow the Black River between Big and Little Manitou on the trail that connects them. It is a beautiful walk, not very strenuous, that takes about a half hour to an hour depending on how often you stop to photograph a wildflower, watch a chattering pine squirrel, or just enjoy the forest solitude.

The trail to Copper Creek Falls is partially obscured by foliage and undergrowth because not many people take the time to hike the 1.5 miles to the northeast corner of Pattison State Park to view this gorgeous waterfall. A quarter mile north of the park's main parking area, County Hwy B turns east off Hwy 35. Take Hwy B a quarter mile to where it makes a 90-degree turn south. At that curve is an old dirt road with a wide gate across it. Park here, out of the way, to access the trail to Copper Creek. You should stop at the ranger station before setting out to talk about the trail and to get directions, because the trail is often hard to follow. The ranger will show you an aerial photograph of the park and will suggest you use a compass for navigation.

The falls is a two-stage cascade that first tumbles down 15 feet of black basalt. The water lands in a shallow basin, then squeezes between two large chunks of basalt and drops another six feet. Potholes formed by water, sand, and time are evident in the sandstone walls on the north side of the cedar-lined canyon, and downstream a hundred yards there are scraps and caverns from an abandoned copper mining operation dating back to the turn of the century. Downstream you can see the fault line where basalt deposits and sandstone meet. It is a fantastic outing; plan to spend at least half a day for the trip to the falls and back. Bring food and water.

Directions: Take State Hwy 35 south from Superior approximately 13 miles until you see the sign for Pattison State Park. (A state park sticker is required to enter the park.) There are two parking areas close to Big Manitou Falls, one on the northeast side of Hwy 35 near the park shelter house, ranger station, picnic area, and campgrounds (the closest place to park near Copper Creek Falls), and the other, a smaller parking lot, on the southwest side of Hwy 35 after you have crossed the Black River. Signs at both parking lots will direct you to the trail that leads to Big Manitou Falls and the vistas. Ask for directions to Copper Creek Falls at the park headquarters, as the trail is not marked.

Little Manitou Falls is 1.25 mile further south on Hwy 35. Another sign will direct you east off the highway to the parking area for Little Manitou. Little Manitou can also be reached by a hiking trail from the main picnic area near park headquarters.

      ♿ ⛺ 🎣 ✗ ⛱ 🚹🚺 ⛷ E,M,S

Amnicon Falls

Amnicon Falls, Amnicon River

Douglas County
Amnicon Falls

Location: Amnicon River 10 miles east of Superior, Amnicon Falls State Park.

Amnicon Falls is actually a series of waterfalls ranging in height from five to thirty feet. The Amnicon River is fed by many smaller streams that give it a curious mixture of colors depending on the time of year and the amount of rainfall or spring runoff. One can see the color of the Amnicon change from a dark, tannic, iron brown to a bright, pinkish red almost overnight at certain times of the year, particularly after a heavy rainfall. This is due to the sandstone and clay soils of the surrounding hills.

A covered bridge connects the riverbank to a small island between the two main falls. From the bridge you can look upstream and see how the river winds around giant boulders and deep pools. In summer, lilies, buttercups, rosehips, and daisies adorn the muddy banks. In the winter the snow is deep, sometimes several feet. During heavy snowfalls the covered bridge is even more inviting and picturesque.

Downstream from the covered bridge the terrain is strikingly different. The river drops suddenly within walls perhaps 50 feet high along the Douglas Fault as the Amnicon takes a quick twist westward and then northward, cutting a deep gouge in the banks where white pines scarcely hold their own in the thin soils.

Directions: From Superior take State Hwy 2 east toward Brule. About 0.75 mile east of the intersection of State Hwys 2 and 53 watch for County Hwy U and a sign directing you to turn north to Amnicon Falls State Park. Take that exit and follow the road about 0.5 mile to the park entrance and the headquarters building where you need to purchase a state park sticker (if you don't already have one). You can begin your outing from this parking area, or you can go to other parking areas to access campsites or trailheads. (Note: the park is closed in winter, but you can walk in to see the falls.)

  ♿ ⛺ 🎣 ✗ 🪑 🚻 🥾 E,M

BAYFIELD COUNTY
Lost Creek Falls

Location: Lost Creek No. 1, one mile southwest of Cornucopia, Bell Township.

Directions: Take U.S. Hwy 13 west from Cornucopia approximately one mile and turn south (left) on Klemik Road, which is a dirt road that is passable without 4-wheel drive from mid-May through September. Stay on Klemik until you reach the ATV/snowmobile trail, about 0.75 mile. A yellow gate on the left hand side is your indication of the trail. Park off to the side and begin following the ATV trail east (left) into the county forest.

🚶🚶M

About fifteen to twenty minutes into the hike you will cross a creek on an old bridge. This is Lost Creek No. 2, not to be confused with the one you are heading for. Another ten minutes will get you to Lost Creek No. 1 and, again, a weathered bridge. From here the trail goes to the right in a sweeping curve and heads gradually uphill. Stay on the ATV trail but watch closely for the footpath that leads from the trail to the waterfall. The footpath is not marked. It will take about five minutes to reach it from the bridge. If you are unsure you can always go back to the creek and follow it upstream to the falls. However, as you approach

Lost Creek Falls on the ATV trail you should be able to hear the rushing water.

Lost Creek Falls is a pearl among Wisconsin's waterfalls. Lost Creek flows gently over a pink and lavender streambed. When the creek reaches the falls it plummets fifteen feet straight down off a fragile sandstone ledge into a shallow pool. If you are careful and watch your step you can inch your way behind the waterfall and look through the cascade. Cliff swallows build their earthen nests under the wet cap of Lost Creek Falls, so it is best not to disturb this area in the spring.

This is true wilderness in the heart of the Bayfield Peninsula. Don't be surprised to see a black bear on your hike to the falls. My wife had a close encounter on one of our hikes into the falls, although she reports the bear was as shocked to see her as she was to see it!

Black bear sow

Lost Creek Falls

Siskiwit Falls, Siskiwit River

BAYFIELD COUNTY
Siskiwit Falls

Location: Siskiwit River, one-half mile east of Cornucopia, Bell Township.

Siskiwit Falls is one of my favorites. It is actually a series of waterfalls that cascade gracefully toward Lake Superior. Siskiwit Falls is one of the state's most beautiful waterfalls, descending in tiny steps over tiers of black shale and sandstone.

At the bridge on Siskiwit Falls Road you can see waterfalls both up and downstream. The falls to the south is comparatively diminutive at six feet but, nonetheless, dazzling. The Siskiwit River flows over the crown of this falls in a rush of frothy water, landing in a pool. The river then flows north underneath the bridge.

Downstream from the bridge the river is perhaps twenty feet wide in most places, its banks muddy and low. Here the river descends quickly in the long chute of the main waterfall down a chiseled bed of black shale, brownstone, and sandstone, every now and then flowing into dark pools where scrappy rainbow trout, brookies, German browns, and coho salmon come to spawn in the spring or fall.

Both sides of the river are tree-lined with overhanging limbs and rocky outcroppings, and at the third waterfall the east wall of the gorge is a sandy cliff. At this point the Siskiwit River pivots almost 90 degrees to the northwest and flows another half mile to the bridge on State Hwy 13 in Cornucopia and then into the harbor.

Directions: Travel north from Washburn on County Hwy C approximately 18 miles until you reach Siskiwit Falls Road. Turn right (east) onto Siskiwit Falls Road, continue an eighth of a mile and then park on either side of the bridge spanning the Siskiwit River. From any corner of the bridge you can descend the bank to the Siskiwit River. The property on both sides of the river is privately owned, so you must walk downstream following the footpath that hugs the river.

  E

BAYFIELD COUNTY
Little Sioux River Falls

Location: Little Sioux River, 3.5 miles north-west of Washburn, Bayview Township.

Directions: The Little Sioux River Falls are on private property. However, you can access the falls by following the Little Sioux River through public lands and Nekoosa Paper Company property, and then wading the shallow stream the last quarter mile until you reach this gradually descending waterfall. Take State Hwy 13 north from Washburn toward Bayfield. Three and a half miles north of Washburn you will cross the Sioux River bridge. Lake Superior will be on your right. Take the first left turn you come to after crossing the bridge, which will be Friendly Valley Road. Stay on this road until you come to another bridge approximately 1.5 miles west. This is the confluence of the Sioux and the Little Sioux rivers. The Little Sioux is the one on your right, or the north side of the bridge. The falls are upstream from the bridge. There is a small parking area on the south side of the road.

Little Sioux River Falls

The Little Sioux River Falls drop 10 feet over brownstone into a round pool at the bottom. The waterfall is gorgeous, and can send a surprisingly large volume of water downstream following a winter with heavy snowfall and after heavy rain. The area is quite wild—don't be surprised if you spot a black bear or other uncommonly-seen wildlife as you push your way to the falls.

Little Sioux River Falls are surrounded by private property on both riverbanks. There is no established hiking trail to the waterfall, but this stretch of the river is popular with trout anglers who have created a path along the muddy banks of the river for about an eighth of a mile as it flows through state-owned property. The next eighth of a mile the banks are private property but you can avoid this property by bearing due west from the state land and entering Nekoosa Paper Company land.

Hike north along the north/south property line a short distance until you meet the Little Sioux River again. You will be able to stay next to the creek now for the next half mile as you head west/northwest, without trespassing, but then you will have to wade the Little Sioux River the last quarter mile to the waterfall. Do not attempt this hike without a good compass and an up-to-date plat book, for you will certainly lose your way through the tangle of tag alder in the dense, wet bush country. This route is definitely for the adventurous. Bring a lunch and a non-leaking pair of waders, and plan to spend the entire day.

The easiest way to view this waterfall is to refer to your plat book and find out who the current landowners are. Knock on their door and ask if they would allow you to cross their land to see the waterfall. If you are turned away you can don your waders and opt for the fun way in!

Chapter 2
ASHLAND COUNTY

As I ascend St. Peter's Dome Trail, I enter a world of tranquillity and beauty, far from the daily pressures of job and city. The trail crosses narrow creeks that intersect the damp footpath, past grand monarchs of hemlock and conifer, around hidden curves that reveal bracken fern in rich greens, goes up and over long drumlins, and crosses kettles that tell of the glacier's path as it pushed over the landscape thousands of years ago.

The view from atop St. Peter's Dome is breathtaking. As I stand on this mammoth pink granite 1600 feet above sea level, the highest point in the Chequamegon National Forest, Lake Superior spreads across the hazy northern horizon, a gigantic sheet of blue. Twenty miles away, amidst the hills of Bayfield County, the tiny town of Washburn is barely visible. Ashland is easier to spot with its smokestacks at the power plant, the lighthouse that stands a mile out in Chequamegon Bay, and the abandoned ore dock that reaches far from shore on the east side of the city. Directly below and to the west, the view is just as incredible, especially in the fall when the panorama is a tapestry of color! Farms and fields, interspersed with pine plantations and a few roads, break the yellows, oranges, and reds.

I watch as the sun drops into the western horizon, and I think how lucky I am to have spent a day here at St. Peter's Dome.

(Left) *Copper Falls, Bad River*

ASHLAND COUNTY
Morgan Falls

Location: South Branch Morgan Creek, 12 miles west of Mellen and 16 miles south of Ashland, Marengo Township.

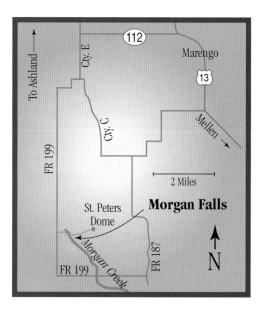

I am frequently asked which Wisconsin waterfall is my favorite, and I invariably answer "Morgan Falls." The hike to Morgan Falls is not long, but the half-mile trail is serene and quite picturesque as it meanders through a glade full of paper birch, ash, and sugar maples. About three-fourths of the way to Morgan Falls you come to the usually shallow waters of the South Branch of Morgan Creek. At times you can see tiny insects and fish in the pools, and fallen leaves from neighboring sugar maples hitch a ride on the surface of the creek and disappear out of sight downstream.

Rounding the last bend of Morgan Creek you come upon Morgan Falls, a slender 70-foot-high cataract that bounces down the mossy face of a gigantic slab of granite. The first plunge is a 64-foot drop onto a concave granite ledge, followed immediately by an 80-degree turn away from the granite wall and the final six-foot drop into the

sand-carved pothole below. Morgan Creek then flows on inconspicuously through a wooded crevasse.

A visit to Morgan Falls should include a trek to St. Peter's Dome, which is more strenuous than the Morgan Falls trail. The trails begin together, then divide. The hike will take you along switchbacks, around several large rock outcroppings, across springs that squirt from fern-covered grottos in the hillside, to the granite knob called St. Peter's Dome, with its magnificent views of the Chequamegon National Forest, the Marengo Valley, and Chequamegon Bay. If you are in shape and maintain a steady pace, you'll reach the top of the dome in 30 to 45 minutes.

Directions: From Ashland, take State Hwy 112 (Sanborn Ave.) south approximately nine miles to the intersection of Hwy 112 and County Hwy E. Hwy 112 will curve 90 degrees east. Hwy E goes south through Sanborn. Turn on Hwy E and travel through four 90-degree curves, watching for County Line Road (Forest Road 199) at the fourth curve. Turn south on County Line Road and stay on it 4.5 miles to the parking area for Morgan Falls and St. Peter's Dome trail.

From Mellen, travel west on County Hwy GG seven miles to FR 187 (Mineral Lake turnoff). The posted sign is not easy to spot as it is on a curve on the south side of the road, so take your time as you get within range and watch for it carefully. Take FR 187 north (the only option), staying on FR 187 through three 90-degree curves, about 4.5 miles, until FR 187 intersects FR 199 at the third curve. Go west and then north on FR 199 approximately five miles to the parking area for Morgan Falls and St. Peter's Dome trail. This route is slow and the roads wind through the Chequamegon National Forest, but it's a gorgeous drive, especially in the fall, so don't let the complicated directions discourage you.

Λ 🏃E,M,S

Morgan Falls, Morgan Creek

ASHLAND COUNTY
Copper Falls
Brownstone Falls
Granite Falls

Location: Bad River, Tyler Forks, three miles northeast of Mellen, Copper Falls State Park.

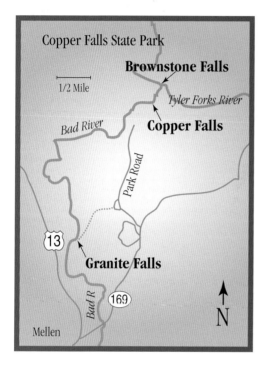

Copper Falls State Park is one of Wisconsin's most beautiful parks. Its ancient red and basaltic lava flows and deep canyons encompass spectacular waterfalls that highlight this fascinating division of the Penokee-Gogebic Range. Many of the buildings, bridges, and stone stairways were built by the Civilian Conservation Corps in the 1930s. The canyon was unsuccessfully explored for copper deposits in the late 1800s and early 1900s.

Copper Falls is a 40-foot waterfall that interrupts the root beer-colored flow of the Bad River an eighth of a mile downstream from the park's log-framed concession building. Recently, the falls began chewing more soil and rock from the eastern bank of the river to a point slightly behind the crown of the falls. This new erosion

has required rerouting the hiking trail on that side of the river.

The river at Copper Falls splits and flows through two crevasses. On the left as you face it, the upper half of the waterfall is slender; it swirls against a heavy shoulder of basaltic lava then out onto a black basalt slab before dropping over the brow of its second stage, doubling in width as it cascades between two giant lava boulders before plummeting into the stony gorge below.

Copper Falls' smaller half (on the right) also churns between slabs of black, basaltic lava, less dramatic than its companion, but every bit as stunning. The two falls rejoin in a pool and the river then flows through a gorge with 60- to 125-foot high walls of sandstone, conglomerate, shale, and sandstone.

Five hundred yards downstream from Copper Falls, the Bad River and Tyler Forks River join. Brownstone Falls, just upstream along Tyler Forks, drops some 30 feet into a craggy pool where the two rivers meet. A wood-railed viewing area overlooks Brownstone Falls. At the confluence of the Bad River and Tyler Forks just below Brownstone Falls stand jagged spires of red and black lava, conglomerate rock, survivors of century upon century of relentless flowing water. The bedrock floor of the canyon here is scoured rock. The two rivers, now joined for the trip to Lake Superior, flow between two sandstone stalagmites called Devils Gate, bounce around a gravel corner a few hundred yards downstream, and vanish into the wilderness.

Directions: From Mellen, travel east on State Hwy 169 approximately two miles and watch for the brown sign with yellow lettering directing you north into Copper Falls State Park. A state park sticker is required and (if you don't already have one) can be purchased at the park's ranger station. The park is open year-round.

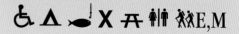

Copper Falls, Bad River

Brownstone Falls, Tyler Forks River

At the south end of Copper Falls State Park as you enter the main gate, Loon Lake is on your left. Its sparkling water is surprisingly chilly, yet swimmers enjoy its beach. Anglers try their luck with panfish, northern pike, and bass, and visitors are often treated to the sight of the bird that gave the lake its name. There is a bathhouse adjacent to the beach, and it is here that you begin the trail that leads to Granite Falls on the Bad River. The path to Granite Falls is a self-guided nature trail that is about two miles round-trip. It takes you through a wonderful forest of red oak, birch, aspen, and conifers.

Granite Falls is not as awe-inspiring as its two counterparts downstream in the park, but the geology of the Bad River here is strikingly different. As its name implies, huge chunks of granite block the river at the falls, which are really more of a rapids than a full-fledged waterfall.

Copper Falls, Bad River

Chapter 3

IRON COUNTY

urney?" I thought, "I've never heard of that town." I wondered how big it was and how many people might be living there. My interest in Gurney was the result of hearing about a beautiful waterfall just south of the tiny town on the famous Potato River. As things turned out, Gurney, the Potato River, and the Potato River Falls were easy to find. Traveling north on State Hwy 169 in Iron County, I spotted the large sign pointing to Potato River Falls just as I was about to enter the city limits of Gurney. A dusty, well-worn country road took me to a shady parking area that proved to be the end of my search.

The clamor echoing through the deep canyon made it clear exactly where the falls were located. Even in the middle of the night one could accurately pinpoint the waterfall.

From my elevated vantage point on the cedar lined, northeast rim of the mineral-rich gorge the slightly chlorinated scent that most large waterfalls exude wafted in my direction from the Potato River far below me. I followed the narrow trail, smelling the highly oxygenated water as I descended. At the bottom, I stood in the river in my neoprene waders, captivated by the overflowing Potato River Falls, caught in the spray that filled the canyon from the waterfall just upstream from me.

I inched downstream along the black ledge toward the smooth crown of the main waterfall, gingerly placing one neoprene-shod foot in front of the other, keeping my balance with the help of a gnarled cedar pole.

Peeking over the crest of the falls toward the bronze-colored pool of water 30 feet below, I noticed a huge, moss-clad snapping turtle, timeless as the river, sunning itself on a chunk of granite near the west edge of the waterfall.

(Left and above) *Potato River Falls, Iron County*

IRON COUNTY
Potato River Falls

Location: Potato River, one mile southwest of Gurney, Gurney Township.

Directions: Traveling east from Ashland, you'll cross the Ashland-Iron County line at the crest of Birch Hill on U.S. Hwy 2. Almost two miles into Iron County watch for State Hwy 169 to the south. There is a sign directing you to both Potato River Falls and Copper Falls State Park. Travel south about 2.5 miles to Gurney, which is a tiny town with only a few houses. Just south of Gurney, not even a quarter mile, is the small billboard directing you to turn west off the highway onto a gravel road that goes one mile to the parking area.

△ ⚓ Χ ⛵ 🚻 🥾 E,M,S

The Potato River Falls is really a trio of dramatic waterfalls that are evenly spaced along 400 rugged feet of the Potato River. The parking and picnic areas are at the top of 150-foot-high red clay cliffs at the bottom of which is the river. From the picnic tables one can see the largest and most spectacular waterfall, which is wider and higher than the two other falls upstream. This is ideal for those who are not physically able to descend the difficult trail for closer encounters with the river.

There are three main hiking trails at the park, all of which begin at the picnic grounds. One is a level and easily navigated path that leads southeast into the adjoining hardwood forest and,

more or less, skirts the Potato River along the cliff far above its banks. Another trail from the picnic area descends a very steep and slippery approach down an eroded crevasse that affords several wonderful vistas overlooking the largest waterfall. At the bottom of this muddy trail you will have to make the decision to either climb back to the top or wade the Potato River, for there is no defined riverbank at this point except during low water conditions.

The third trail is also quite steep but the trek is improved with wooden stairs that traverse the hillside down to a rocky platform that allows easy viewing of the two upstream waterfalls.

The first of the three waterfalls gushes 20 feet down a sloping chute of smooth bedrock into a swirling pool. The river then flows against the exposed sides of four huge boulders on its way to the second waterfall and another 20-foot drop. Below those falls, the river turns first west, then northwest again, and flows 200 feet to the top of the last falls, where it plunges 30 feet over a black lava shelf into the pool below.

Foster Falls, Potato River

Foster Falls, Potato River

IRON COUNTY
Foster Falls

Location: Potato River, five miles north of Upson, Gurney Township.

Directions: From the intersection of State Hwys 77 and 122 in Upson, travel 5.2 miles north on Hwy 122 and turn left (west) on Sullivan Road. The road is not signed, but it is the only obviously navigable road off that stretch of Hwy 122. Go west on Sullivan Road 2.9 miles and you will see the Potato River in front of you where it washes out Sullivan Road. You cannot proceed westerly even though your highway map says Sullivan Road continues. A hundred yards before the river there is a dead-end dirt road heading north. Take that road two hundred yards to the end. Park there and walk the few steps down to the falls. (See map p.27)

Foster Falls is a lovely waterfall in a remote area of dense upland woods, river bottoms, and lowland timber. The drive to Foster can be an adventure in itself; Sullivan Road is never passable before May 1. Even in summer it can be a challenge bouncing through the ruts and side-swiping overhanging limbs. But once you arrive at the Potato River you will find the trip was worth the effort.

The Potato River drops quickly and splits in two as it flows over Foster Falls. On the near shore the cascade is a series of three eight-footers. At the bottom, this half of Foster Falls joins the 30-foot-high falls from the far side of the river. The wind created by the waterfalls is tremendous, and spray fills the air and drenches the shoreline.

The Potato River continues toward Potato River Falls. A hundred yards downstream on the left, a lagoon captures woody debris and heaves it up on the banks in a mountain of logs, branches, and stumps. This is a spectacular area, wild as any territory in Wisconsin.

IRON COUNTY
Wren Falls

Location: Tyler Forks River, five miles northwest of Upson, Anderson Township.

From the time you turn off Sullivan Road and go the last 1.3 miles, you will get several glimpses of Tyler Forks River as it pokes its way downstream. Along the route you will notice aspen and birch felled by beaver on the high banks of the river, their leafy tops all pointed down in the same direction. At the falls, the Tyler Forks narrows to a few feet wide and its banks rise about forty feet. The sudden drop and constriction causes a loud roar even though Wren Falls drops only 15 feet. The thick pillar of tannin-hued water shatters the pool below, creating a blend of colors somewhere between your favorite lager and a milk shake.

You can climb down into the gorge (be careful!) along the stony bank on the near side of the river 50 yards downstream from the waterfall. At the bottom you can then walk back upstream to a point just 15 feet from the base of the cascade.

Directions: If Sullivan Road near Foster Falls was not washed out by the Potato River these directions would be simpler. However, you must start at Upson and travel west on State Hwy 77 for 2.9 miles to Casey Sag Road. Turn north and stay on Casey Sag Road 5.25 miles to where it intersects Sullivan Road. Sullivan Road is **not signed**. You can turn right here and go 0.9 mile for a view of Foster Falls from the west bank of the Potato River. Or, turn left for Wren Falls and drive 1.8 miles on Sullivan Road, where you will see Sullivan and Vogues roads meeting at the tip of a V. Vogues Road is **not signed**. At this point you will see a brown sign at the head of an unsigned road to the south indicating a cooperative venture between the Iron County Forest and the Department of Natural Resources. That road leads to Wren Falls. Follow it 1.3 miles to a fork. Park and walk the right fork to the top of the hill where you will hear the falls. The walk from your vehicle to the falls is 0.2 mile. (See map p.27)

Wren Falls, Tyler Forks River

IRON COUNTY
Upson Falls

Location: Potato River in Upson, at the Upson Community Park.

Directions: Upson is located approximately 10 miles southwest of Hurley. Take State Hwy 122 into Upson and go four blocks to Upson Park Road. Turn left (west) and follow the road two blocks to the park.

Set against a backdrop of spruce, oak, and hickory, and blessed with an enormous number of basalt boulders scattered across its fifty-foot width, Upson Falls is a beautiful cascade with fast water and deep pools. The falls are in two stages. The upper falls, which are a few feet wider, roll gently down a six-foot drop into a pool surrounded by sand and gravel banks. From this pool the river flows to the narrower lower falls, with their nine-foot drop. From a vantage point below the lower falls looking eastward, the two stages appear as one continuous waterfall.

Upson Park has picnic tables, a shelter, a water pump, and toilet facilities. The park is wooded with hills to the south and west and Upson Falls on the eastern edge. The trail to the falls is easy to locate and is well worn. It takes about a minute to walk to the waterfall. In fact, you can see Upson Falls from the parking lot.

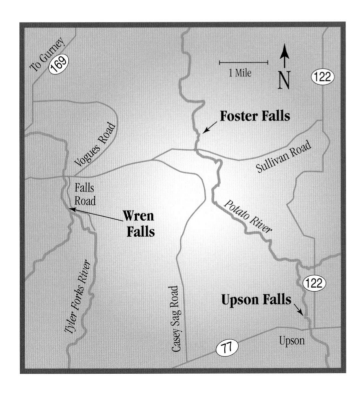

Wren Falls, Tyler Forks River

Superior Falls, Montreal River

IRON COUNTY
Superior Falls

Location: Montreal River, 15 miles northwest of Hurley, Saxon Township.

Directions: Take U.S. Hwy 2 west from Hurley 11 miles toward Ashland. When you come to State Hwy 122 turn north (right) and follow it 4.5 miles, where you cross the Montreal River bridge into Michigan. Turn left at the second gravel road after the bridge where a sign directs you to the falls and the parking area. Leave your vehicle at the power station and take the well-worn footpath 150 feet to the caution fence that runs a short distance along the east rim of the canyon. DO NOT cross this wooden railing; a fall into the 100-foot-deep gorge would be fatal. (See map p.30)

 E,S

For a waterfall that has been robbed of most of its power by diverting 75% of the river flow behind an upstream dam, Superior Falls is stunningly beautiful and should be included in a tour of falls in the Hurley area.

The Montreal River canyon encompasses surging rapids framed by birch and conifers that cling to the rocky slopes. Superior Falls drops abruptly through a 150-foot polished rock channel in the riverbed. In the sides of the cliff on the east side of the Montreal River you can see light brown igneous rock eroded and layered in sharp, flat platforms that give the impression of footholds should someone foolishly attempt to descend the ravine to reach the river. The safe way to reach the river is to follow the marked Flambeau Trail from the northeast end of the parking area to a fantastic overlook of Lake Superior, and then climb down a rough, narrow path to the sandy shore of the lake. From that point you can walk along the bank upstream for a closer encounter with Superior Falls.

The mouth of the Montreal River is legendary for spring and fall angling for steelhead (rainbow) and German brown trout.

Superior Falls, Montreal River

IRON COUNTY
Saxon Falls

Location: Montreal River, 13 miles northwest of Hurley, Saxon Township.

Directions: Take U.S. Hwy 2 west from Hurley, turn north on State Hwy 122, and watch for County Hwy B after two miles. Turn right (east) onto Hwy B and travel 1.7 miles to a four-way intersection. Turn left (north) and go 0.4 mile. There, the road forks right and left. Turn right and drive downhill on a dirt road 0.6 mile to the power dam and parking area. The left-hand road, also dirt and gravel, takes a short hop over the crest of a low hill, then descends a couple hundred yards to a power plant and a parking area.

Almost 90% of the water that used to flow over Saxon Falls has been diverted for electric generators. Even so, Saxon Falls is an impressive cascade that plummets 75 feet in a deep canyon on the Montreal River.

There are two ways to view Saxon Falls. From the power dam parking area walk west following the signs that read "Danger, Falls Ahead." Cross the Montreal River on a steel-railed walkway attached to a huge black water pipe (it's got a sign indicated that it's for viewing the waterfall) and continue about 0.25 mile on the Michigan side of the river to an overlook above Saxon

Falls. Below and to the west you will see a set of stairs leading to a riverside power plant, a bridge crossing the Montreal River, and a steep set of stairs that climb out of the gorge on the Wisconsin side of the river. Unfortunately, on either end of these stairs is a locked gate—the stairs and bridge there are for employee access only.

The view from the Wisconsin side of the Montreal is quite spectacular as well, but is partly blocked by trees that grow thick on the walls of the gorge. Park your vehicle at the electrical transformer station and walk into the woods toward the sound of Saxon Falls. Less than fifty yards of hiking will get you to a suitable spot to view the falls. How wonderful it would be to have seen Saxon Falls in its full glory before the dam robbed it of so much power!

Saxon Falls, Montreal River

Peterson Falls, Montreal River

IRON COUNTY
Peterson Falls
(Also called Interstate Falls and
Montreal Falls)
Unnamed Falls

Location: Montreal River, one mile northwest
of Hurley.

Directions: Take U.S. Hwy 2 west from
Hurley, go through the interchange, and go
about an eighth of a mile further and turn
right on the first unnamed road you come to.
There is a sign that reads "Nasi Ero
Construction Co." A glance north from Hwy 2
will reveal one of their company buildings.
Follow this unnamed road to its end, approximately 500 yards, and park off to the side of
the turn-around. The trail is on the north side
of the cul-de-sac. Follow it to Peterson and
Unnamed Falls.

 E

The hike to Peterson Falls is not all that long,
between a quarter and a half mile, but the surrounding lowland woods is inviting, cool, and
somewhat mysterious, with moss and vines drap-
ing the hemlock, cedar, and tamarack. Much of
the narrow path is muddy or soft, as the clay
underfoot tends to give way with each step you
take.

Peterson Falls plunges 35 feet onto a huge
chunk of quartzite that obviously broke off from
the main body of rock beneath the waterfall
sometime in the distant past, then spills over several smaller boulders before crashing into a deep
lagoon. You can reach the lagoon by taking the
trail beyond the waterfall and then following the
flat bank, or you can lower yourself down the
steep banks close to Peterson Falls using the
trunks of cedar trees to slow your descent.

After some time at Peterson Falls, you can follow the wet and rocky banks of the Montreal
River upstream roughly 0.5 mile to Unnamed
Falls. Although the drop in the stream there is
only a few feet, Unnamed Falls is well worth the
small investment in time to locate, particularly in
the spring when the snow is melting, causing a
rush of water down the river.

Sit for a few moments atop a chunk of dry
stone on the riverbank and listen to the surge of
water. If you are not sure where your original
path into the forest can be located from this
point, simply walk west a few minutes and you
will meet the trail that takes you back to your car.

IRON COUNTY
Gile Falls
Rock Cut Falls

Location: Gile Falls is located about two miles southwest of Hurley on the West Fork of the Montreal River. Rock Cut Falls is located approximately four miles north of the town of Montreal on the same river.

Gile Falls has lost about 50% of its flow because of a power dam that diverts water at the outlet of the Gile Flowage. Gile Falls is surprisingly noisy for its small size. The river is only eight feet wide here, and the falls are only 10 feet high. The river bounces between boulders that dot the riverbed, then swirls under an ATV bridge. The land here is privately owned.

The property surrounding Rock Cut Falls is also privately owned. However, a three-mile ride west from Hurley on the Ironhorse Trail aboard an ATV or snowmobile will provide opportunity for you to view Rock Cut Falls where the trail crosses a former railroad bridge. A map showing the Ironhorse Trail, as well as all other ATV and snowmobile routes in Iron County, is available through the Iron County Chamber of Commerce or the Wisconsin Department of Natural Resources.

A canoe or kayak excursion to Rock Cut Falls is a more thrilling way to see this wonderful cascade, but before attempting the trip check with the employees at the dam in Montreal to see if the flood gates are open or closed. Either way it is possible to float the river, keeping in mind that this can be a very challenging venture over predominantly grade III rapids in the spring, and grades II-III rapids in mid-summer.

Put in at the small park on the north side of Hwy 77 across from the Montreal city hall, and plan to take out at the bridge crossing the West Branch of the Montreal River located about 3.5 miles west of Hurley on U.S. Hwy 2.

At first the river ride will seem easy even though the current is strong. About 2.5 miles downstream is a railroad bridge. Paddle to either shore and scout the best course if you intend to run the next set of rapids. Once you paddle into this section of the river there is no turning back

or getting to shore for a normal take-out. There are two drops to watch for, and both should be scouted from shore.

If you elect to portage around these rapids take out on the right side of the river and follow the railroad tracks about 150 yards around the curve going west. Once you have passed the rapids, launch your vessel and continue your adventure.

A mile downstream from the railroad bridge you will see a small park on the left shore and at about the four-mile point you will see a steel bridge looming in the distance. It is there that you first hear the thunder of Rock Cut Falls.

The waterfall can be run by canoe or kayak, but it has a high hazard rating. Take the time to scout before attempting these falls. Rock Cut is a 15-foot waterfall but it drops gradually enough through a 150-foot stretch of river to allow an expert to safely navigate it. The view from the Ironhorse Trail below Rock Cut is breathtaking, and hundreds of snowmobilers stop in winter to take in the magnificent panorama.

The remainder of the ride takes you through steady grade II and III rapids. Be careful and be aware of the limits of your skills. At the five-mile mark you will come to the Hwy 2 bridge which is your take-out point.

Directions: Approximately two miles southwest of Hurley on State Hwy 77 is the small town of Montreal. Look for Kokogan Street to the south about mid-way through town. Turn left and go half a block to Mellen Street. There is a trail on the west side of Mellen Street that leads to Gile Falls. However, the property is owned by Angelo Lupino Construction Company and you must ask permission to use the trail.

An alternate access is located on the west side of the river. Turn into the Montreal City Hall driveway (across the bridge one block west of Kokogan Street). Park at the rear of the lot and walk 0.2 mile on an ATV trail to the Montreal River and Gile Falls.

The map labels include:

River Road · West Fork Montreal River · Town Park Road · Kimball Drive · 2 · N · 3/4 Mile · Center Drive · **Rock Cut Falls** · Iron Horse Trail · Hurley · 77 · Montreal · Gile · City Hall · Trail · Mellen St. · Kokogan St. · **Gile Falls**

Rock Cut Falls, West Fork, Montreal River

Spring Camp Falls, West Fork, Montreal River.

Spring Camp Falls

Location: West Fork Montreal River, eight miles southwest of Hurley, Pence Township.

Directions: Take State Hwy 77 southwest from Hurley to County Hwy C, which is on the outskirts of town. Turn south on Hwy C and drive 2.5 miles, crossing the Gile Flowage causeway, and continue another 1.5 miles to where Hwy C makes a 90-degree turn due east. At that point there will be an unnamed dirt road heading directly west toward the Gile Flowage. Take that dirt road exactly one mile and you will come to a three-way intersection and another 90-degree turn to the south which will be East Branch Road, the one you want. Stay on East Branch Road approximately 2.7 miles until you come to another unnamed dirt road on your right that takes you west 1.1 mile to the waterfall. You will not be able to see or hear the waterfall from the parking spot, but a narrow path directly off the end of the road will take you up a short hill through the woods 100 yards where you will be able to hear Spring Camp Falls.

 **X** M

Named for its use first by Ojibwa Indians and later by lumberjacks, Spring Camp Falls provides an isolation that is perfect if you want to get away from the stress of a crowd and be by yourself in the great outdoors. I have been to Spring Camp Falls often and there's never been anyone else there at the same time.

The West Branch of the Montreal River flows out of Island Lake eight miles southwest of Spring Camp Falls. It picks up speed, energy, and water from several feeder creeks. By the time the Montreal reaches Spring Camp Falls the river is running swift and full, creating an exciting cascade that drops about 20 feet between a gently pitched basaltic ledge to the west and a higher, steeper stone embankment on the east side of the river.

A hundred yards downstream from Spring Camp Falls is a small island made up of boulders dropped by the glaciers. This island traps all sorts of debris, particularly large broken tree trunks and twisted branches that float down the Montreal in the winter and spring. Sometimes a pile is stacked a few feet high against the face of the island and along the shore, waiting for the high water that will shove everything farther downstream.

Chapter 4
POLK, SAWYER, PRICE, EAU CLAIRE
AND MARATHON COUNTIES

When I was a teenager growing up in Madison, my friends and I were occasionally allowed to take fishing trips up north. On those trips, I always thought of Wausau as the "line of demarcation" where northern Wisconsin really began. I still feel that way when I travel through Wausau and Marathon County with its rolling hills covered with birch, aspen, ash, maple, and oak. I fight a walleye to the boat in the soft current of the Big Eau Pleine Reservoir in spring or roam the Dells of the Eau Claire River in search of the key that will unlock its mystery.

This day the Eau Claire River is undergoing the special cleansing that comes with severe drought. The flow is scarcely enough to cover the riverbed as it meanders around outcroppings of granite and conglomerates, picking up speed only long enough to flow into small pools that line the center of the river in no apparent order.

To the untrained eye this tiny flow might be a disappointment. But the observant visitor sees an opportunity to explore every crack and crevasse of the exposed bedrock and contemplate the slow, continuing power of flowing water. But the moment must be snatched before the rains come and the river channel is once again hidden from view.

(Left) *Cascade Falls, Osceola Creek*

Cascade Falls, Osceola Creek

POLK COUNTY
Cascade Falls

Location: Osceola Creek, Main Street (State Hwy 35), downtown Osceola.

Directions: In downtown Osceola, Osceola Creek passes underneath the highway bridge and flows west towards the St. Croix River. Ample parking along Main Street allows quick access to the path leading to the falls. A sign marks the path.

The historic city of Osceola is located on bluffs overlooking the St. Croix River, a National Wild and Scenic Riverway. Excursion steamboats

in the late 1800s made regular stops where Osceola Creek meets the St. Croix River. Passengers disembarked and hiked a boardwalk along the creek to the base of 25-foot Cascade Falls. The boardwalk is gone, but a newly constructed pathway leads to the same breathtaking destination. The waterfall is particularly stunning in fall when the panorama of bright colors is at its peak. When the creek reaches the crown of the waterfall it spreads flat across the lip and then showers down over a layered limestone and sandstone ledge.

Cascade Creek drops 110 feet from the outlet of the Osceola Mill Pond upstream from Cascade Falls, over the falls, and through a wooded ravine to the St. Croix River.

(Right) *Big Falls, Eau Claire River*

EAU CLAIRE COUNTY
Big Falls

Location: Eau Claire River, nine miles east of Eau Claire, Seymour Township.

Directions: Take County Hwy Q (Olson Drive) east from Eau Claire approximately nine miles to the intersection of Hwy Q and South 110th Avenue. A sign at the intersection directs you south into Big Falls County Park. Big Falls is southeast of the parking lot; the trailhead is obvious and the walk is only a couple hundred yards on an asphalt path. A similar parking area and path are located on the opposite side of the river. To reach it, keep going east on Hwy Q from 110th Avenue two miles to County Hwy K. Turn south on Hwy K and go 1.5 miles across the Eau Claire River. Immediately on the south side you will see a sandy road to the right. Follow this road to the parking lot. It's a short walk to the falls.

Big Falls is so close to metropolitan Eau Claire that it is probably one of the most frequently visited waterfalls in Wisconsin. On hot summer days flocks of swimmers, waders, and sunbathers linger in the cold waters of the Eau Claire River. They plop themselves on, below, and behind the waterfall. Every rock that will hold a body has one. It looks much like a seal colony. A better time to photograph Big Falls and to enjoy it in solitude is from the beginning of October through the end of April.

The river rounds a sharp bend on its final approach to the narrows that form Big Falls. Eons of erosion has cut a 50-foot-wide gash through glacial deposits, forming this 25-foot-high waterfall. Millions of gallons of water per hour flow across the polished boulders in the riverbed at Big Falls' crest, then drop into a deep pool below.

The Eau Claire River is a splendid fishery. There are several boat launching sites between Eau Claire and Big Falls, but the launch directly below the waterfall will only accommodate boats that can be carried in.

Big Falls, Eau Claire River

Dells of the Eau Claire, Eau Claire River

MARATHON COUNTY
Dells of the Eau Claire

Location: Eau Claire River approximately 15 miles east of Wausau, Plover Township.

Directions: Take County Hwy Z east from Wausau 13.5 miles to the intersection of Hwy Z and County Hwy Y. There you will see a sign that reads "Eau Claire Dells County Park 1 3/4 Miles." Turn north and follow Hwy Y to the park.

The Dells of the Eau Claire County Park is a genuine jewel. The park sits on a rocky cliff overlooking an elongated, boulder-strewn riverbed

carved in rocks left by ancient volcanoes that stood a mile high above the site two billion years ago, and by a glacier that left rocks, sand, and debris behind 10,000 years ago. Included within its 190 acres are hiking trails, scenic overlooks, foot bridges, 25 campsites, a swimming beach, picnic areas, playgrounds, and two shelters.

The descent of the riverbed from the Hwy Y bridge to a point roughly 800 yards downstream is quite spectacular. Along the route massive boulders of pinkish-gray rhyolite scattered across the width of the river create drops of two to ten feet.

The rhyolite formations are etched with ancient potholes. These round, smooth basins were carved by sand and stones that twirled and agitated for thousands of years in eddy currents in the depressions. Some of the potholes are five feet in diameter.

In early to mid-May the forest floor in the park comes alive with a sea of pure white trillium,

Pothole, Dells of the Eau Claire

Jack-in-the-pulpit, spring beauty, bloodroot, and pink lady slipper. Birds of the warbler, finch, and sparrow families are busy collecting thatch for nesting material, and small animals can be seen gathering seeds and repairing their burrows after a long, cold winter. A few deer browse the red oak, yellow-bud hickory, and basswood and, if you are lucky, you will see a doe chewing a mouthful of fresh grass while her spotted fawns follow close behind.

possible to visit the falls in a wheelchair. However, the grade is fairly steep and should be attempted only with assistance. About 100 yards down the trail the path forks; to the right you can hike 0.5 mile to Slough Gundy; to the left the trail will take you 200 yards to the 10-foot-high Little Falls. The waterfall is located at one of the widest and most open areas on the South Fork of the Flambeau. A long, thick bank of granite divides the flow into two narrow chutes, creating lots of pressure as the river flows over the falls.

OTHER FALLS

SAWYER COUNTY
Little Falls

Location: South Fork Flambeau River, 9.5 miles north of Hawkins, Winter Township.

The hiking trail that leads down to Little Falls and Slough Gundy is black-topped, making it

Directions: Take County Hwy M north from Hawkins through two, 45-degree curves and watch for a sign on the left side of the road at about the 9.5-mile mark that reads "Little Falls Slough Gundy Scenic Area." Turn left into the small parking area, then follow the trail at the west end.

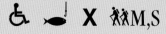

PRICE COUNTY
Big Falls

Location: Jump River, 10 miles south of Kennan, Kennan Township.

Directions: From Kennan travel south on County Hwy N about 9.5 miles to the intersection of Hwy N and Big Falls Road where you will see a sign that reads "Big Falls County Park." Turn right (west) and go one mile, then turn left into the park. The parking area for the falls is just a few yards into the park.

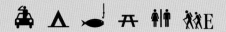

At Big Falls, the Jump River descends 30 feet in a series of frothy cascades that drop from one pool to the next. Big Falls, at about eight feet, is the largest drop in the series. The bank on the park side is scattered with boulders. The opposite shore is a clay bank about 50 feet high. Fishing is excellent below the falls where anglers try for walleye, northern pike, musky, and suckers. The park at Big Falls offers camping, fresh water, a shelter, picnic tables and grills, and toilets. This stretch of the Jump River is also excellent for kayaking, with grades II-IV rapids in spring.

EAU CLAIRE COUNTY
Hamilton Falls

Location: North Fork of the Eau Claire River 25 miles east of Eau Claire, Wilson Township.

Directions: Follow County Hwy Q east from Eau Claire 13 miles to County Hwy X. Turn right (south) on Hwy X and go 0.5 mile to County Hwy D. Go left (east) on Hwy D to the small town of Wilson where Hwy D turns north and meets County Hwy DD. Turn onto Hwy DD for 0.25 mile and watch for County Hwy G. Stay on Hwy G almost two miles and then turn onto County Hwy MM and go one mile to Hamilton Falls Road. Turn right (south) on Hamilton Falls Road. A weather-beaten sign at the corner reads "Hamilton Falls Road, Town of Wilson, Memorial Park 1/2 Mile." In early spring there might be a "closed" sign on this drive if it's too muddy to navigate. Otherwise, most vehicles can make it to the falls which is 2.3 miles from the intersection.

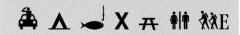

The North Fork of the Eau Claire River flows through an S curve at Hamilton Falls across a 75-foot-wide granite outcrop, then drops six feet before continuing downstream. An easily-navigated sandy trail descends 40 feet from the road to the shoreline. You can see Hamilton Falls from your vehicle. You'll pass Memorial Park, a fine place for a picnic, on your way to the falls.

Chapter 5
FLORENCE AND MARINETTE COUNTIES

Squinting into the dense aspen forest, I could not imagine where the thunderous waterfall I could hear so plainly could be, for the terrain in every direction was heavily wooded and mostly flat. But I knew the unmistakable rumble was real. The roar reverberated off every rock and nook in the canyon to the south, which I could not yet see.

A two-foot-wide path meandered in and around low growth of wild raspberry and blue chicory, and I apologized to myself when I accidentally stepped on a booted amanita and its stem broke off in the brown humus. The low, throaty thunder of the waterfall intensified as I moved closer, reminding me of a symphony orchestra rolling through the introduction of a masterpiece by Beethoven or Bach.

Approaching with caution, I could see the cut in the earth where Long Slide Falls flowed from its bed of calcareous shale and black limestone. The small, sharply tipped leaves on the aspen and birch in the river gorge quivered and waved in the quiet but continuing breeze created by the flowing water. I found a partially hidden deer trail that would allow me a closer view of Long Slide. I followed the switchback down the slippery canyon wall until I stood near the base of the waterfall. I carefully eased along the slippery, moss-covered rocks of the riverbed. The raw, untamed power rushing at me filled me with so much energy that at times I quivered in my waders. It was like being recharged after being on "low" for too long.

(Left and above) *LaSalle Falls, Pine River*

FLORENCE COUNTY
LaSalle Falls

Location: Pine River, eight miles southwest of Florence, Commonwealth Township.

Directions: From Florence, take County Hwy N south approximately nine miles to the intersection of Hwy N and County Hwy U. From this point continue south on Hwy U for 0.5 mile, where you will meet County Hwy C. Turn west on Hwy C and travel 1.8 miles through two 90-degree curves and watch for a small wooden sign on the left side of the road facing east that reads "LaSalle Falls." Another wooden sign on the north side of Hwy C reads "Entering Florence County Forest." Turn north on the unsigned dirt road (LaSalle Falls Road) just past the Florence County Forest sign. The road immediately forks; take the road to the left and stay on it for 2.4 miles until you come to the parking area for the falls. The trail begins there.

The hike into LaSalle Falls is wonderfully invigorating. Though only moderately difficult, it is longer (almost a mile) than most trails to Wisconsin's waterfalls. Along the way you may see and hear a variety of bird and animal life, including the northern three-toed woodpecker, brown creepers and nuthatches, tree and ground squirrels, and chipmunks. Maybe you'll be as lucky as I was, and see a baby porcupine waddle across the trail!

As you walk along the well-worn, sometimes-moist path and get closer to the falls, you will notice a light breeze start to whisper through the tops of the sugar maples and the quaking aspen. Just then you will begin to hear the roar of the falls. The Pine River will appear down below between the trees that line the walls of the 100-foot-high chasm. Follow the trail along the ridge. It gradually descends to a viewing spot just ten feet above the 20-foot-high falls.

One of the curiosities about LaSalle Falls is its continuing high water flow throughout the year, regardless of extremes of rain or drought. As you face LaSalle Falls from below you will notice a 35-foot-tall tower of granite, squared off on three sides, that leans north to the edge of the Pine River.

Misicot Falls, Menominee River

MARINETTE COUNTY
Sand Portage Falls
Misicot Falls
Unnamed Falls

Location: Menominee River, two miles southeast of Niagara, Niagara Township.

Directions: From Niagara go south on U.S. Hwy 141 to U.S. Hwy 8. Turn left (east) on Hwy 8 and cross the Menominee River into Michigan. Drive another 2.5 miles and watch for the "Piers Gorge Scenic Area" sign. Turn left onto the paved Piers Gorge Road and drive to the fork in the road. Stay to the left and follow the road to the end, about a mile. The trail begins there.

 E,M

The Piers Gorge Natural Area is a magnificent natural preserve along the Menominee River. Its name is derived from the rock formations that in places stick out into the river like piers. Four major piers can be seen along the maintained trail that follows the river to the north a mile and a half from the parking area. It is wide and can accommodate a wheelchair. Be careful when approaching the river as the flat rock is slippery even when dry.

The trail passes underneath a dense growth of red and white cedar, over a couple of wooden foot bridges, and soon you come to the first pier (all four are marked along the trail by tall wooden poles) and an unnamed waterfall about two feet high, one of several along the walk. The unnamed falls are where the river is widest, from 100 to 200 feet across. From the first pier most people in wheelchairs cannot continue, as the hill ahead is too steep.

About twenty minutes into the hike, depending on your speed and how often you stop to enjoy the river, you will come to Misicot Falls. Your vantage point 70 feet above the river gives you a great vista from which to view its eight-foot plunge. Misicot Falls was formed due to the shape of the gorge here. At this point the rock formation on the west shore juts out into the river, forcing the water to flow in an area only

49

Misicot Falls, Menominee River

half as wide as the river upstream from the rock. A break in the rocks in the riverbed creates a chute into a deep hole on the far side, providing a path over the falls for river rafters. As their rubber rafts dive over the falls the passengers squeal with fear and delight; copious amounts of water spill into the raft, and everyone is soaked. (The rafts continue downstream through a smaller set of rapids then bounce into another set of S curves that end at a spot where the riverbank is a rock wall that towers at least 75 feet overhead.)

Near the end of the hiking trail, past a set of power lines that run straight up a steep hill, you come to a 30-foot-high outcropping of granite overlooking the river. Climbing to the top to get a better view, you will see an island upstream; the river divides to flow around it. The main channel flows over a set of rapids. The smaller right channel makes a gradual loop, curves around the east side of the island, then drops over five-foot-high Sand Portage Falls. It is a pretty cascade, the dark water sliding between several jagged boulders that stand glistening in the frothy water.

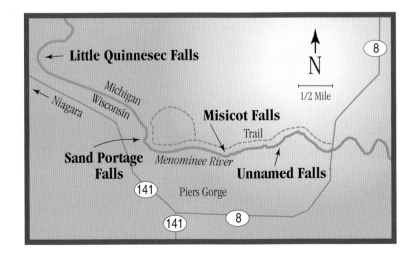

MARINETTE COUNTY
Smalley Falls

Location: North Branch Pemebonwon River, six miles northwest of Pembine, Niagara Township.

Directions: From Pembine go north on U.S. Hwy 8/141 about five miles and turn right (east) on Morgan Park Road. Follow this road 0.5 mile until you come to the signed driveway for Smalley Falls. Take this drive 0.1 mile to the turn-around and park. If the road is too rutted or muddy park on Morgan Park Road and hike into the falls. The trailhead is marked. (See map p.53)

Smalley is my favorite in this part of the state, with a sensational drop of nearly 50 feet down a gradual grade. The trail leading into the waterfall is flat for a few yards near the parking area but then descends quickly toward the river.

The ravine is usually in shadow, hidden from the sun by 40-foot-high granite walls. Atop them a concentrated growth of white cedar further blocks the sun, at least until afternoon when it shines directly down on Smalley Falls.

In the Smalley Falls gorge is a large group of rocks that fell into the Pemebonwon thousands of years ago. In the large shallow hole in the wall of the gorge left after the rocks broke away, bracken fern and multicolor gill polypores thrive in the moist confines of a shadowy plant community among rotting trunks of cedar and oak. The largest chunk of rock released from the south wall rests in the center of the stream, and the water climbs up this love seat-sized boulder several feet before flowing around it on both sides. The sweet aroma of natural chlorination emanates from Smalley Falls, and it is fun to sit quietly on one of the rocks nearby and watch as thousands of gallons per minute roll by.

Smalley Falls, North Branch Pemebonwon River

(Left and above) *Long Slide Falls, North Branch, Pemebonwon River*

MARINETTE COUNTY
Long Slide Falls

Location: North Branch Pemebonwon River, seven miles northeast of Pembine, Niagara Township.

The short, wide path leading to Long Slide Falls is an easy walk through low-hanging stems of wild raspberry, blue chicory, and trillium. It takes you to a rocky ledge overlooking the 50-foot-high falls where the river drops over large hunks of shale, sandstone, and granite.

Spring is the best season to visit Long Slide Falls if you want to hear the roaring falls at its peak. The rocky banks are completely engorged with white frothy water surging into every nook and crevasse on its rush downward. It is chilling (literally) to stand and absorb the mist and splatter at the bottom of the falls while looking up toward the relative calm at the top of the rocky funnel.

The gorge at Long Slide Falls is not protected by railings or barriers. Be careful here, especially if you have kids along. Several trails lead up and downstream from Long Slide, and a couple of them go down into the ravine below the falls. Again, use caution if you approach the falls from below. From the top of Long Slide there is a 1.5-mile-long trail that leads west to Smalley Falls. It is a great hike through a magnificent forest.

As is the case with many of the rivers of Marinette County, the Pemebonwon flows into the Menominee River on the Wisconsin-Michigan border.

Directions: From Pembine travel north on U.S. Hwy 8/141 about five miles and turn right (east) on Morgan Park Road. Follow this road 1.6 miles until you reach the driveway for the parking lot at Long Slide Falls.

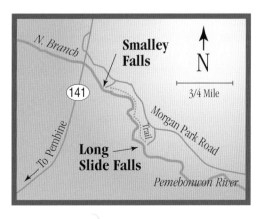

Pemene Falls, Menominee River

MARINETTE COUNTY
Pemene Falls

Location: Menominee River, 12 miles east of Beecher, Beecher Township.

Directions: From Beecher take County Hwy Z approximately 10 miles to the Menominee River. Cross the river into Michigan (the road becomes CR 374) and then turn left (north) on the first sand road (V-4) east of the bridge and stay on it for 1.1 miles. The third dirt road to the left will lead you to the parking area for the falls with a sign that reads "Pemene Falls." You can also reach the falls from the Wisconsin side of the river by turning north on Verhayen Lane just before the bridge that crosses the Menominee River into Michigan. Go 1.3 miles to where Verhayen Lane narrows. From there a path leads 400 yards to the waterfall.

Flowing over an abandoned and partially destroyed dam, Pemene Falls carries the Menominee River around cement abutments then drops 10 feet into the rocky channel below. Jagged stone lines the riverbanks, its surface covered with soft, slippery sheets of moss and lichen.

The Menominee River is a phenomenal fishery for many species, including walleye, musky, bass, and northern pike.

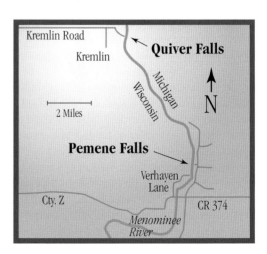

Dave's Falls
Bull Falls

Location: Both of these waterfalls are located on the Pike River approximately 0.5 mile south of Amberg, Amberg Township.

Directions: Dave's Falls County Park is located 0.25 mile south of Amberg on the west side of U.S. Hwy 141. Watch for the white billboard directing you into the park. To get to Bull Falls turn east on County Hwy K, 0.5 mile south of Amberg and follow it 0.3 mile to the power lines that cross the road. Walk north down a moderately steep slope following the power lines 200 yards to the Pike River and Bull Falls. (See map p.57)

Dave's Falls County Park encompasses two unique waterfalls and spectacular scenery. Plenty of parking is provided, and picnic tables dot the wooded park.

A short trail leads north from the parking area up a gradual incline with wooden steps and rail-ings. At the summit the enchanting voice of the Pike River fills your ears, and a few more stairs down the other side take you to a rock outcropping overlooking the main waterfall. The cascade drops perhaps 30 feet. At the bottom a swift current flows around chunks of black and gray rock. A sign downstream warns swimmers of the dangerous undertow; the Pike has taken four lives below Dave's Falls. Use extreme caution when exploring the riverbed here.

A variety of wildflowers and ferns speckle the forest in the park. The beautiful setting is a photographer's dream. Immediately after a rainstorm is a perfect time to catch the dark green glint on the edges of bracken fern or the stark white trillium flowers that pop from the wet humus on the forest floor. Nowhere in Wisconsin will you witness such a wild arrangement of flora, fauna, rock, and water in as neat a package.

A few hundred yards west of Dave's Falls a wooden foot bridge spans the Pike River. Within view of the bridge is the 15-foot-high upper falls. A path follows the shore right next to the upper falls.

Bull Falls, downstream from Dave's Falls, is another exciting waterfall that surges between walls of weathered boulder and clay that constrict the riverbed and cause a corresponding increase in the river's speed just as it plunges 15 feet into the rapids below.

Dave's Falls,
Pike River

MARINETTE COUNTY
Chipmunk Falls

Location: North Branch Pike River, approximately 2.5 miles northwest of Amberg, Amberg Township.

Directions: The section of the Pike River where Chipmunk Falls (also known as Chipmunk Rapids) is located runs through private property and is inaccessible by land. Floating the rapids is the only way to experience Chipmunk Falls.

The North Branch of the Pike River in Amberg Township is loaded with rapids and squat waterfalls that dance to the ever-changing tunes of the river. Tubing, canoeing, and kayaking are popular ways to enjoy the Pike. Almost any bridge as it crosses the Pike can be used as an access point, depending on how much of the river you want to see and how much time you have to invest in the trip.

Chipmunk Falls is a grade II-III rapids that drops about six feet during spring and early summer, varying in height according to the rainfall. (Be sure to scout the falls if you run them during high water.) The falls are reached within twenty minutes if you launch at the bridge on French Road two miles north of Amberg. The river here flows out of the Twelve Foot Falls area, down through the Marinette County Forest. Chipmunk Falls is but one of the many thrills you encounter in a day's outing. Take out about three miles south at Dow Dam Road. There will be three more sets of unnamed rapids before then, all grades I and II.

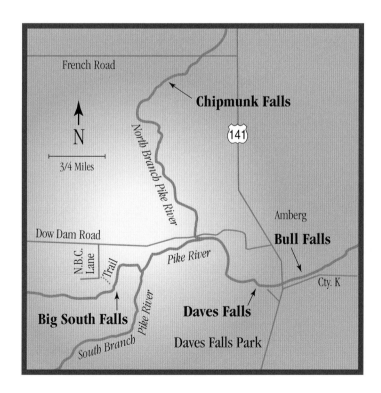

(Left) *Dave's Falls, Pike River*

Bull Falls, Pike River

Bull Falls, Pike River

MARINETTE COUNTY
Bull Falls
Three Foot Falls

Location: North Branch Pike River, five miles southeast of Dunbar, Dunbar Township.

You may have to look hard for the abandoned logging road that takes you to Bull Falls; this will be an adventure that will be a test of your woods lore. The road you parked on is really a big loop that makes one more 90-degree curve up ahead and comes back out on Twelve Foot Falls Road. At the first curve where you are now parked look straight east and find the logging road.

The hike begins on county forest land but ends on private property. If you take this hike early in the morning expect wet clothes from the mist and dew that clings to the ferns and blackberry bushes that push in on the path. The hike is slightly down-hill and should take about ten minutes. When you

Directions: Approximately three miles east of Dunbar on U.S. Hwy 8 you'll come to Lily Lake Road. Before the intersection is a sign directing you to Twelve Foot Falls County Park. Take Lily Lake Road south 1.5 miles to a four-way intersection. Turn right onto Twin Lakes Road (unmarked), following the signs for Twelve Foot Falls County Park. Drive 0.5 mile to Twelve Foot Falls Road and turn left (south), following the sign for Twelve Foot Falls County Park. Travel one mile and watch for a narrow dirt road leading east into the pine forest. This will be the second driveable dirt road on your left you will come to on Twelve Foot Falls Road. Turn east and drive 0.1 mile to a 90-degree curve and park off to the side. An unused logging road, grown over with ferns, leads east 0.3 mile to the Pike River and Bull Falls. (See map p.61)

🚶🚶M

reach the river you will see a house and a huge yard on the other side. As you near the river you will hear two things: The grumble of Bull Falls and the bark of the property owner's dog from across the stream. Don't worry, the canine cannot cross to your side. The property owner will not yip, either, if you are there to view the falls and are not hunting.

Bull Falls is boisterous even during summer low water. The river here is about 30 feet across and Bull Falls drops seven feet in a series of rapids, flowing over small boulders and woody debris.

If you now walk the banks of the Pike River downstream approximately 0.25 mile, you come to an oxbow that creates Three Foot Falls, a quick skip over a handful of scattered stones. The countryside surrounding this small cascade is breathtaking and is more of a justification for finding this secluded spot than the waterfall itself.

Another way to reach Three Foot Falls is to go back to your vehicle after your call at Bull Falls and continue on the same dirt road to the next 90-degree curve. There you will find a rustic camping spot in the county forest on the riverbank, just off on the edge of the lane. Park and walk down to the Pike River through the campsite. Three Foot Falls will be 200 yards upstream.

Eighteen Foot Falls, North Branch, Pike River

MARINETTE COUNTY
Eighteen Foot Falls
Twelve Foot Falls
Eight Foot Falls

Location: North Branch Pike River, six miles southeast of Dunbar, Dunbar Township.

Directions: Approximately three miles east of Dunbar on U.S. Hwy 8 turn south on Lily Lake Road. Just before this intersection you will see a sign directing you to Twelve Foot Falls County Park where these three waterfalls are located. Take Lily Lake Road 1.5 miles to a four-way intersection. Turn right, again following the sign for the county park. You will be traveling on Twin Lake Road (unmarked); go 0.5 mile to the sign directing you south onto Twelve Foot Falls Road. The turnoff and small sign for Eighteen Foot Falls is two miles down Twelve Foot Falls Road. Turn east onto the narrow dirt road as the sign indicates and go 0.3 mile to the parking area. The trailhead is on the northeast side of the clearing.

Almost one mile south of the Eighteen Foot Falls turnoff is the road leading into Twelve Foot Falls County Park. It is well marked and easy to find. You must pay a fee at the entrance. Both Twelve Foot Falls and Eight Foot falls are in this portion of the park within a five-minute walk of each other.

The short but winding trail leading into Eighteen Foot Falls is partially hidden by overhanging ferns and sumac and is heavily laced with scattered shards of granite. Careful, the trail is rough and slippery. Eighteen Foot Falls is approximately as high as its name implies. At the base a pool with a soft, marl bottom is fine habitat for crayfish, trout, and mayflies that usually appear on the surface of the river in late May to early June.

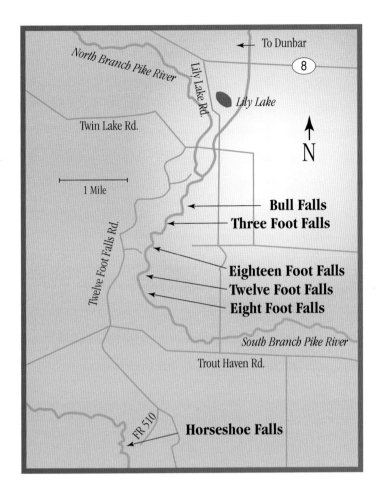

The canyon surrounding the falls is heavily vegetated; the strong roots of pine and cedar hold fast to the river's edge. Below the cascade is a wide basin; then the river divides and flows in two separate courses around a long island of sand and marsh grasses, reuniting on the south side.

A mile downstream from Eighteen Foot Falls is Twelve Foot Falls, situated in the center of Twelve Foot Falls County Park. This beautiful cascade can be viewed from the paved parking lot a hundred yards to the west. Campers in the park are often seen early in the morning sitting along the banks or atop the rocks surrounding the lagoon below the falls, some of them fishing or taking pictures, others pondering and enjoying nature. The pond here can be amazingly still, encircling trees sometimes reflected on the clear surface.

South of the parking lot is one of two campgrounds in the park. A short walk behind this campground brings you to Eight Foot Falls. The scene is different here despite its close proximity to Twelve Foot Falls. The crown of the falls is on flat, smooth granite that directs the flow of water eight feet down into a crystal-clear basin. The stream is not very wide at this point and the banks on each side are open.

Downstream an old, fat willow stands alone on a car-sized island. In mid-July hoards of dragonflies congregate on this tree and perch on its weathered, gnarled branches.

Twelve Foot Falls, North Branch, Pike River

Eight Foot Falls, North Branch, Pike River

MARINETTE COUNTY
Horseshoe Falls

Location: South Branch Pike River, eight miles southeast of Dunbar, Dunbar Township.

Directions: Approximately three miles east of Dunbar on U.S. Hwy 8, turn south on Lily Lake Road and go 1.5 miles to a four-way intersection. There, you will see a sign pointing toward Twelve Foot Falls County Park. Turn right onto Twin Lakes Road (unmarked) and follow it 0.5 mile to Twelve Foot Falls Road. Turn on Twelve Foot Falls Road and go to the end, about three miles, where you will intersect Trout Haven Road. From the stop sign look across the road, slightly to your right, and you will see a dirt road leading southwest into the forest. At the beginning of this road is a sign directing you to Horseshoe Falls. Follow this road 1.6 miles; you will come to another sign directing you to the falls on Marinette County Forest Road 510. Go 0.5 mile on FR 510 to yet another sign for the falls and turn right. The parking area is 0.25 mile. The trailhead is obvious. The falls are a two-minute walk. (See map p.61)

Flowing in a horseshoe bend in the river, this waterfall is an effervescent charmer situated in magnificently desolate territory deep in the Marinette County Forest. The trail to the falls is easy and short, but hundreds of exposed roots from trees near the path will slow your progress. As the trail ends, your first view of Horseshoe Falls is directly up the main chute, which drops about 10 feet over a 100-yard stretch, ending in a rocky basin.

Goldenrod

Horseshoe Falls, South Branch, Pike River

Big South Falls, South Branch, Pike River

Big South Falls

Location: South Branch Pike River, 1.5 miles west of Amberg, Amberg Township.

Directions: From the baseball field on Amberg's west side take County Hwy V for 1.7 miles to Nutt Road and turn right (west). Take Nutt Road 1.9 miles to Mathis Road and turn right (north) again, staying on Mathis Road 0.9 mile to Dow Dam Road where you will turn right (east). Travel Dow Dam Road 0.9 mile to N.B.C. Lane and turn right (south), following the gravel road 0.5 mile to the dead end where you must park your vehicle. Straight ahead you will see a couple of posts blocking the road and a yellow sign. This is not the path you want to take. Instead, look to your left (east) and see a white sign that reads "Wild River Project—Walk in Access." Take this trail to Big South Falls, about a five- to ten-minute hike. (See map p.57)

 ⨝⨝M,S

My favorite time to hike to Big South Falls is early in the morning, when the dew coats every twig and leaf along the trail. Among the plants you can see are mock Indian paintbrush, oxeye daisy, black-eyed Susan, common mullein, milkweed, wild strawberry and, very rare indeed, the stalks of scouring-rush.

The trail winds downhill almost all the way to the Pike River. The last few yards are the steepest as the hillside is covered with a thick stand of white cedar and spruce that grow up along the river bank, blocking your view until you step past the last trunk and onto the green, spongy terrace.

Big South Falls, which descends 10 feet over a 100-yard stretch of river, is a grade II-III rapids in the spring and early summer, much the same as Chipmunk Falls on the North Branch of the Pike River.

MARINETTE COUNTY
Strong Falls

Location: Peshtigo River, nine miles south of Goodman, Goodman County Park, Silver Cliff Township.

Directions: About 2.5 miles east of Goodman on U.S. Hwy 8 turn south on Parkway Road and go 8.8 miles until you reach a sign that reads "Goodman Park" with an arrow pointing west. Turn here (Benson Lake Road) and go one mile to Goodman Park Road. Turn south (left) here and drive 0.3 mile to the park entrance. You must stop at the entrance and pay a fee.

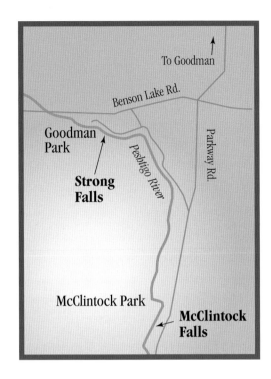

At Goodman Park, three small islands are connected by log footbridges. Between each island is a waterfall that drops about 20 feet. Below the waterfalls the river is wide and deep. It attracts game fish like German brown, brook, and rainbow trout, northern pike, and small-mouth bass. Across the river is seemingly endless forest. In autumn the maple and birch leaves become a kaleidoscope of colors. The undersides of the aspen leaves turn a rich, satiny silver, and the edges stand out in sharp contrast against the clear blue sky.

On your side of the river are the park buildings and campgrounds. Here you will find ample parking, campsites, shelters, drinking water, picnic areas, playgrounds, and toilet facilities.

Blue flag

Strong Falls, Peshtigo River

Veterans Falls, Thunder River

Veterans Falls
Three Foot Falls

Location: Thunder River, 14 miles northwest of Crivitz, Veterans Memorial Park, Stephenson Township.

Directions: From Crivitz take County Hwy W west 10.2 miles and turn right (north) onto Parkway Road. Follow Parkway Road 3.1 miles to the Veterans Memorial Park entrance. There is an entrance fee; the parking area is just ahead. Two trails lead down to the waterfalls.

    ♿ Δ 🎣 ✗ ⛏ 👫 🚶‍♂️E

A trail of flagstones from the parking area leads to where the Thunder River rushes under a wooden footbridge. Just downstream from the bridge, Veterans Falls drops 15 feet, smashing through a narrows in the stony chasm and tumbling over shiny rocks. The water pours into a murky lagoon below the falls and slows before flowing on toward Three Foot Falls.

On hot summer days there may be dozens of swimmers below Three Foot Falls, cooling off in the river as it bounces off rock ledges.

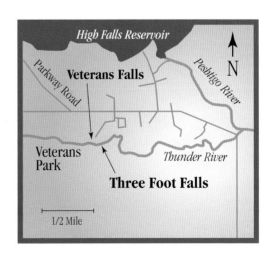

OTHER FALLS

FLORENCE COUNTY
Meyers Falls
Bull Falls

Location: Pine River, approximately 10 miles west of Florence, Florence Township.

The Goodman Tract, which is open to public use, was once the largest managed forest in Wisconsin. Even though a lot of logging has taken place within this forest it is still lush and thickly wooded. Meyers Falls is at a spot where the Pine River squeezes between rows of gray boulders that line the banks. The falls has a seven-foot drop that is most impressive during spring runoff. At Bull Falls the river narrows and drops five feet. Both Bull and Meyers falls are excellent sections of the Pine River to fish for brook and German brown trout throughout the spring and summer. The Pine River is excellent for canoeing; novices can portage around the waterfalls. For the more advanced canoeist almost all the rapids and some of the waterfalls on the Pine River are navigable, although some of the rapids are class III during spring high water.

Directions: Drive west from Florence 2.5 miles on State Hwys 101/70. Continue west on Hwy 70 for 5.5 miles to the Goodman Grade Road (unmarked). Go south on the Goodman Grade 2.2 miles until you reach the Pine River. Park here and ford the river (a pair of waders is a good idea). The riverbed is solid, laden with baseball-size and smaller rocks. Once across the river walk south 0.2 mile to the first four-way intersection. Turn right (west) and go 0.75 miles to Meyers Falls, or turn left (east), and walk 0.6 mile to Bull Falls on the logging road. At that point the trail to the river is not very obvious. A very small sand pit, the size of an average kitchen, on the north side of the logging road is your clue that the trail is nearby. Just beyond the pit is the path leading downhill to Bull Falls. When anglers are using the trail during fishing season it is easier to find, as many arrive on ATVs.

An alternate route from the north is available if the Pine River is too deep to ford. From Hwy 70 take the Goodman Grade one mile. At that point a logging road bisects the Grade. Turn right (west) and drive 1.35 miles to Meyers Falls, or turn left (east) and go 0.9 mile to Bull Falls. This access is a logging road that may be impassable at times. You can leave your vehicle parked on the side of Goodman Grade and hike to either falls.

FLORENCE COUNTY
Jennings Falls

Location: Popple River, nine miles southwest of Florence, Fern Township.

Jennings Falls is really a rapids, but in spring the water pushing through this constricted neck of granite can be quite amazing. The slender waterfall cascades down a gradual descent of about 10 feet. During periods of high water Jennings Falls is a grade III rapids. It is advisable to scout Jennings Falls if attempting to paddle it; your portage should be made on the right (south) bank to avoid dragging your craft and gear over the steep cap of granite on the north side.

Even though the falls itself may not be as spectacular as some other waterfalls in the state, the hike to it ranks very near the top. Try it in the fall, or on snowshoes in January.

Directions: Take State Hwy 101/70 for 2.5 miles west from Florence. Turn south on Hwy 101 at the intersection where the highways split. Follow Hwy 101 for six miles and watch for Mulberry Lane an eighth of a mile west of the bridge over the Pine River. Turn south on Mulberry Lane and go 0.5 mile. Go left through the curve at the end of the lane and park so you are not blocking the swinging gate you will see there. From that gate a dirt road leads to the south through private property. You are welcome to access Jennings Falls on this path if you respect the landowner's generosity and do not hunt along the walk.

Follow this road 0.6 mile and you will see a small, shingled cabin on your right. Go past the driveway that leads up into the cabin. A hundred yards beyond the road forks. The fork in front of you (to the right) turns into a grassy lane with a tire-track trail. Follow this grassy road 0.35 mile to where it ends. A narrow path leads from this cleared area to the falls, which you will hear at this point. Be careful approaching Jennings Falls as the cliff overlooking the river is high, slippery, and covered with dense vegetation.

Paper birch bark

FLORENCE COUNTY
Washburn Falls

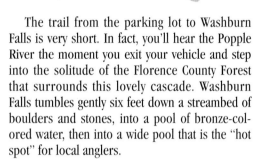

Location: Popple River, 11 miles southwest of Florence, Fern Township.

Directions: From the LaSalle Falls parking area (see p. 48) go west on LaSalle Falls Road 2.4 miles to an old wooden sign that reads "Washburn Falls, 1 1/2 miles" with an arrow pointing south. (A half mile before this sign there is another dirt road leading south. This is White Birch Road. It is not marked. Be sure to continue west at this intersection, do not turn south on White Birch Road.) The sign directing you 1.5 miles to Washburn Falls is missing its top right-hand corner and bushes are growing around it. Follow the arrow on the sign, south. You will now be on White Ash Road. Note that, while the sign says Washburn Falls is 1.5 miles, in fact, the waterfall parking area is 1.8 miles. You will understand how important this information is when you visit Washburn Falls. The road is rough and rutted, impassable in early spring. It is an ATV route so be on the lookout.

The trail from the parking lot to Washburn Falls is very short. In fact, you'll hear the Popple River the moment you exit your vehicle and step into the solitude of the Florence County Forest that surrounds this lovely cascade. Washburn Falls tumbles gently six feet down a streambed of boulders and stones, into a pool of bronze-colored water, then into a wide pool that is the "hot spot" for local anglers.

The Popple River flows out of sight 100 yards to the northeast as it rounds a muddy bend where several weeping willows hang over the shore. Tall, green marsh grasses creep to the edges of the brown banks, and yellow marsh marigolds speckle the dense undergrowth. In mid-summer dragonflies hover and zip over the surface of the water; if you stand very still they will light on your arm and rest their wings for a moment before buzzing off.

Ground squirrel

FLORENCE COUNTY
Big Bull Falls

Location: Popple River, 15 miles southwest of Florence, Fence Township.

Directions: Take State Hwy 101/70 for 2.5 miles west from Florence, turning south on Hwy 101 at the intersection where the two highways separate. Follow Hwy 101 for 10.8 miles and watch for West River Road crossing Hwy 101 from the west. Turn west on West River Road and go 0.6 mile to a small parking area and a sign that reads "Falls Parking." Take the hiking trail on the south side of the road 0.2 mile to the falls.

Located on state property, Big Bull Falls is a favorite among trout anglers. Spunky brook, brown, and rainbow trout inhabit the deep, cold holes below the falls and provide exciting adventure for the flycaster or worm soaker. The Popple River in this spot splits to flow around a small, wedge-shaped island. The south channel is a fast grade III rapids that plummets over a series of short rock ledges. This channel can be navigated by canoe. The north channel is too nasty to challenge in a canoe.

FLORENCE COUNTY
Little Bull Falls

Location: Popple River, 18 miles southwest of Florence, Fence Township.

Directions: Little Bull Falls is not accessible by public road as it is completely enclosed by private property. However, the falls can be reached by canoe from several spots upstream, depending on how much time you want to invest. Best times are April, May, and early June.

The shortest paddle is from the bridge on Morgan Lake Road. Take State Hwy 101 south from the intersection of Hwys 101 and 70 west of Florence. Travel approximately 14 miles to the intersection of County Hwy C and Hwy 101. There, Hwy C goes east and Morgan Lake Road goes west. Take Morgan Lake Road through the Town of Fence and continue west 1.5 miles to where Rock Creek Road and Morgan Lake Road merge. Go north 0.5 mile to a Y intersection. Stay to the left (west) on Morgan Lake Road and drive through beautiful hardwood and pine forests to the Popple River. Park a second vehicle at the boat landing under the Hwy 101 bridge just south of West River Road. This will give you a wonderful run of four miles over the six-foot drop of Little Bull Falls, Big Murphy Rapids, Nine-Mile Rapids, and Big Bull Falls. This stretch of the river is very scenic, heavily wooded, and can be managed by intermediate or novice paddlers. Most of the rapids here are grade II except during spring high water.

OTHER FALLS

Quiver Falls

Location: Menominee River, 10 miles east of Pembine, Pembine Township.

Directions: A half mile north of Pembine on U.S. Hwy 8/141, turn east on Kremlin Road and go nine miles to the uninhabited berg of Kremlin. As you pass through town you will come to an intersection of three roads; keep going straight, cross a railroad track, and the road will fork. Stay to the left and follow the road about one mile to the parking area. A dirt path will lead you upstream 0.25 mile to Quiver Falls. (See map p.54)

Little Quinnesec Falls
(Kimberly Clark Falls)

Location: Menominee River, City of Niagara.

Directions: Coming into Niagara from the south on U.S. Hwy 141 you will see the Menominee River on your right. Follow the river a few blocks into town and keep going until you come to the Kimberly-Clark Paper Mill. Just before the mill there is a parking lot that is usually used for big trucks. You can park in this lot temporarily. Walk upstream about 400 yards to see the falls. (See map p.50)

The property surrounding Little Quinnesec Falls is all private and there is not a great place to view the falls. Even after you hike along the Menominee River and find a place to partially view the falls, you have to cross private property to get in a better position. However, the walk is good exercise and you might be in town anyway for a picnic at one of several sites along the Menominee River, or to dine at one of Niagara's cafes. Fishing is outstanding below the mills on the Menominee River with northern pike and walleye topping the list of game fish in the river.

The Menominee River just upstream from Quiver Falls is split in two by a small island in the center of the river, forming two long stretches of rapids with the steeper drop of eight feet located on the Wisconsin shore. The other channel, on the Michigan side of the river, is a more gradual descent. Near the base of the falls the saturated, brown ends of wooden pilings poke up through the surface where a railroad track or dam connected Wisconsin to Michigan at one time.

McClintock Falls

Location: Peshtigo River, 12 miles south of Goodman, McClintock County Park, Silver Cliff Township.

Directions: About 2.5 miles east of Goodman on U.S. Hwy 8 turn south on Parkway Road. Go 11.8 miles to the McClintock County Park entrance. A fee is required to enter the park.

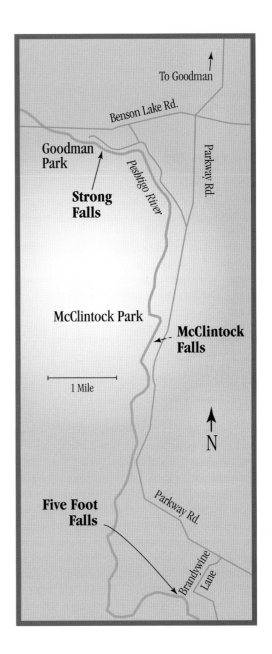

The main feature at McClintock County Park, besides some of the most scenic campsites in Marinette County, are the many rapids, ranging from grades II and III in the spring to grades I and II in the summer. The falls here are best early in the year just after the snowmelt. As the river enters the park, its rocky bed makes a series of short drops. These drops, and the hundreds of small- to medium-sized boulders distributed randomly in the riverbed as it flows through the park, make navigation challenging here.

McClintock Park is also noted for its footbridges connecting several islands. The main bridge, near the parking area, is one of the tallest foot bridges you will find in a county park in Wisconsin. It arches over the Peshtigo River at a 75-degree angle and stands 40 feet above the water at the peak of its arch.

MARINETTE COUNTY
Five Foot Falls (also known as Roaring Rapids)

Location: Peshtigo River, 16.5 miles south of Goodman, Silver Cliff Township.

Directions: From the entrance to McClintock County Park take Parkway Road 4.5 miles south until you come to Brandy Wine Lane. Turn west and take Brandy Wine Lane 1.6 miles to an iron gate on the right side of the road and an ATV trail. Park off to the side and walk the ATV trail (about 0.75 mile) to Five Foot Falls.

On a hot summer day you will have no problem locating Five Foot Falls, for the laughter and squealing echoing from the Peshtigo River will guide you to this set of grade III rapids where tubers bob in the standing waves. The walk to the falls is a gradual downhill on a wide, clear trail.

Five Foot Falls in winter is much more serene. It's a beautiful, quiet trip on snowshoes. The majesty of the pristine forest enveloping the Peshtigo River is unforgettable. In the distance you may hear the yelp of a coyote on a hunt, or was that a timber wolf contacting the clan? A small ermine, now in its white winter coat, escapes the sharp eye of a kestrel that glides over the river in search of a midday meal. Which reminds you to head back to the road and a steaming cup of cocoa.

Porcupine

Chapter 6
MENOMINEE, SHAWANO, AND BROWN COUNTIES

The Wolf River is so vital to the well being of east central Wisconsin, that if it became suddenly unusable it would mean a complete change in the life of everything that lives in its valley, humans included.

The river begins at the marshy outlet on the southern tip of Pine Lake in Forest County, seven miles northwest of Crandon. It twists and turns through forest and swamp, picking up speed and volume. The growing river flows through a corner of Oneida County, then, resupplied by another dozen or so creeks and streams, enters central Langlade County.

When the Wolf enters Menominee County it flows through a series of rapids and waterfalls. It becomes calmer as it flows into northern Shawano County and along the western boundary of the city of Shawano. Below Shawano the river twists and turns, still increasing in volume, takes a short dip into Waupaca County, then back across the southwest corner of Shawano County, and into Outagamie County.

The river here is straighter, its shallows a haven for spawning walleye, northern pike, and both largemouth and smallmouth bass. In April and May thousands of boats, anchored in the steady current, carry anglers trying their skill and luck at catching these elusive game fish. In November the river is lined with freezing duck and goose hunters who huddle behind camouflaged enclosures with their black gun barrels peeking out, pointed to the sky.

South of New London in Waupaca County the river turns north and heads through the heart of town, then makes its final descent through more marsh and low woodland, confined by miles of earthen dikes. The river widens and flows into and out of Lake Poygan in Winnebago County, passes through the quaint village of Winneconne, and ends it journey in Lake Butte des Morts.

(Left) *Sullivan Falls, Wolf River*   *Marsh marigolds*

Evergreen Falls, Evergreen River

MENOMINEE COUNTY
Evergreen Falls

Location: Evergreen River, approximately 32 miles north of Shawano, Menominee Indian Reservation.

The Evergreen River is a tributary of the Wolf River. At 15 feet average width the Evergreen is canoeable, and Evergreen Falls must be portaged due to a huge, jagged rock that sticks up from the gravel streambed.

The falls drop about eight to ten feet, depending on the time of year. It is a picture-perfect waterfall with root beer-colored water coursing through a rocky chasm surrounded by white cedar, birch, and red pine. Early in spring the riverbank is dotted with brilliant yellow marsh marigolds set against a backdrop of green Parry's primrose. Remains of crayfish strewn along the sandy banks are evidence of the otter and mink that flourish along the muddy, grassy banks of the Evergreen River.

Directions: From Shawano take State Hwy 55 twenty-five miles north to Indian Route 3 (shown as County Hwy WW on some maps), turn left (west) on Rt 3 and travel 1.7 miles to Evergreen Falls Road, which is not marked. There is a stop sign at the intersection and another sign that reads "Danger, trucks hauling." Follow this road three miles, being careful to avoid straying left at a fork you come to 0.9 mile along the way. At the three-mile mark you will see a half-acre red pine plantation on your right and a dirt road going north into the plantation. This road leads 0.2 mile to Evergreen Falls. There is a turn-around at the end. The river is a few steps from the parking area. (Note: This is Menominee Indian land. You may park to hike in and view the falls, but you may NOT hunt or fish.)

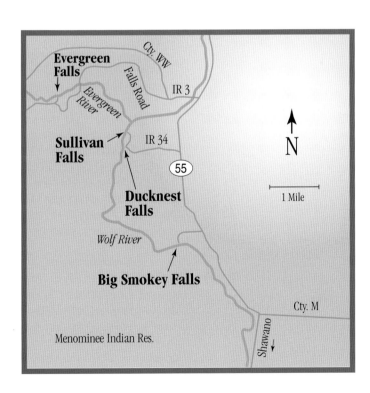

Sullivan Falls, Wolf River, Menominee Indian Reservation

MENOMINEE COUNTY
Ducknest Falls
Sullivan Falls

Location: Wolf River, about 24 miles north of Shawano, Menominee Indian Reservation.

Directions: On State Hwy 55, go north from Shawano 21.5 miles to Indian Route (IR) 34. Follow IR 34, a dirt road bordered by intermittent rock ledges, 1.2 miles to Ducknest Falls and 1.7 miles to Sullivan Falls. (See map p.79)

As soon as you turn off the engine at the parking area near Ducknest Falls you will hear the roar. Follow the sound through the low woodland of dense willows and tag alder to the table of sedimentary rock that encloses both sides of the river. This gorge holds the 300-foot-long rapids that culminate with the six-foot plunge of Ducknest Falls. The river here is thick with boulders, and dangerous souse holes are common.

Ducknest is a waterfall only from late winter through mid-spring when the river is fed by melting snows and spring rain. The rest of the year Ducknest is a grade III-IV rapids and is extremely challenging to the kayaker or canoeist.

A half mile further into the forest, where IR 34 ends, is Sullivan Falls. Park and walk to the edge of the Wolf River to enjoy the seven-foot drop of Sullivan Falls. Although this waterfall must be portaged by canoeists and kayakers, a four-hour raft journey from Shotgun Eddy upstream will take you safely over Sullivan Falls, Ducknest Falls, and Big Smokey Falls.

MENOMINEE COUNTY
Big Smokey Falls

Location: Wolf River, 20 miles north of Shawano, Menominee Indian Reservation.

Directions: From the village of Keshena in the Menominee Reservation, go approximately 10 miles north on State Hwy 55 to the intersection of Hwy 55 and County Hwy M. Stay on Hwy 55, go two more miles, and look for a sign that reads "Big Smokey Falls." Three-tenths of a mile further north on the west side of the highway you will find the entrance on a one-way road and another sign that reads "Enter, Wolf River Rafting." This is Indian Route 53. Take IR 53 approximately 0.6 mile to the parking area near the banks of the Wolf River and Big Smokey Falls. (See map p.79)

At Big Smokey Falls the Wolf River is split into two separate waterfalls by a small island that is reached by a bridge from the shore.

As you cross the 30-foot bridge the right-hand portion of Big Smokey Falls cascades underneath, down 25 feet of erratic boulders left by ancient ice movement. This half of the waterfall is a natural collection area for tree limbs that come down the Wolf during spring runoff, and can cause quite a nuisance to the bridge. Menominee tribal members have spent more than one spring repairing the bridge.

The little island is dotted with maples and red pines, and it only takes a minute to stroll to the island to see the other half of Big Smokey Falls.

That half is approximately the same height as the right-hand falls, but the drop is more abrupt with fewer chunks of rock to trap debris. Rafters floating the Wolf use this half of Big Smokey because the rafts don't fit under the bridge over the other half. Big Smokey Falls is the last of four waterfalls that the rafters run; the ride is especially exhilarating on a hot July or August day and, speaking from experience, you *will* get soaked!

Big Smokey Falls, Wolf River

MENOMINEE COUNTY
Big Eddy Falls

Location: Wolf River, 13.5 miles north of Shawano, on the Menominee Indian Reservation.

Directions: From Keshena Falls (see p.85) go north 5.5 miles on State Hwy 55. The unmarked road into Big Eddy Falls will be on your left just past a trailer house. The road into the falls is rocky and heavily rutted. Your best bet is to park off the highway and walk in 0.2 mile to the waterfall. The road is sometimes hard to find. If you get to Indian Route (IR) 53, you've overshot. So turn around and go back 5.1 miles on Hwy 55. The unmarked road will now be on your right.

🚶🚶M

At Big Eddy Falls the Wolf River is three times its normal width. Big Eddy is a double waterfall with a rocky island separating the two halves. The west side of the falls crashes down 10 feet, while the east side (the side nearest the access), plunges eight feet.

This is a fantastic place to sit and view the falls, the river, the shore, and the sky. Sit quietly atop the pink-gray granite glittering with specks of quartzite and enjoy the movement of the river. Perhaps you'll see the flight of a pair of eagles or a lone osprey, the wig-wagging of a muskrat's tail in the water, or the spiny dorsal fin of a northern pike in the shallows below the rocks. Feel the warmth of the afternoon sun as it heats the boulder. You will begin to understand the spiritualism of the Menominee People and how they view special places like Big Eddy Falls.

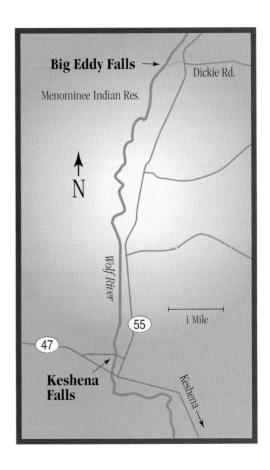

(Right) *Big Eddy Falls, Wolf River*

Keshena Falls, Wolf River

MENOMINEE COUNTY
Keshena Falls

Location: Wolf River, eight miles north of Shawano on the Menominee Indian Reservation.

Directions: Travel north from Shawano on State Hwy 55/47 through the village of Keshena. A mile and a quarter north of Keshena the highway forks; stay on Hwy 55, go another 0.25 mile and watch for a paved road to your left just past the reservation highway garage and gauging station. That's County Hwy C. Turn left and you'll see a bridge over the falls just down the road.

On this stretch of the Wolf River nine miles south of Big Smokey Falls, the swiftly flowing river is forced through a bottleneck in the bedrock. The river here gradually drops 20 feet as it flows through the bottleneck, creating spectacular turbulence. Just below the bridge the falls rush around a tiny island. Everything growing on the small burp of land leans in the same direction as the river's course; most of the roots are partially exposed on the upstream side. In spring the rushing torrent nearly swallows the island; in summer it reappears.

Keshena Falls is surrounded by roads, making it easy to view from a vehicle. Below the falls, the Wolf River flows south under the bridge on Highway 47 and continues toward Shawano.

BROWN COUNTY
Wequiock Falls

Location: 4.5 miles northeast of Green Bay in Wequiock County Park.

Directions: Take State Hwy 57 northeast from Green Bay (toward Door County). Wequiock Park is situated in the triangle where Hwy 57, Bay Settlement Road, and Van Lanen Road intersect. The park is on your left as you travel northeast. There is a sign on the right side of the highway.

For a waterfall that has no obvious source of water other than the New Franken Swamp three miles south, Wequiock Falls has a surprising flow of water over its 25-foot drop. The narrow creek is unnamed, but the charming cascade tumbles with amazing volume into the bowl-shaped pool below. From there, where the now-turbid waters slide over layers of sandstone and sandy shale, the stream regroups and picks its way over moss-covered rocks, flowing northwest to empty into Green Bay a mile south of Point Sable.

The park and picnic area is located on the south side of the waterfall. Bathrooms, picnic tables, and an old hand-operated water pump make this a lovely place to sit, enjoy a picnic in the shade, and listen to the sound of Wequiock Falls a few yards away. On the north side of the park, where Bay Settlement Road crosses a bridge running north and south, a set of stone steps leads to the base of the falls. Watch your step, as the stones may be slippery. Once you reach the floor of the gorge the waterfall is a few steps to the south.

The waterfall is also lovely in winter, when it freezes into an abstract sculpture.

Wequiock Falls can be viewed from your car by driving over the bridge on Bay Settlement Road, and there is wheelchair access on pavement that used to be part of old Hwy 57.

OTHER FALLS

SHAWANO COUNTY
Alexian Falls
Ziemers Falls (also called Gilmer Falls)

Location: Red River, 2.5 and 3.5 miles east of Gresham, in Herman and Richmond townships.

The Red River isn't as well known as some other Wisconsin rivers. Don't let the lack of attention fool you; segments of the Red River have turbulent, challenging rapids. It is best to schedule your float during the spring or early summer, as the stream becomes quite a bit shallower as summer progresses. Grade I and II rapids can be expected during spring high water. Launch at the power dam below Lower Red Lake east of Gresham approximately two miles upstream from Alexian Falls. You will recognize the approach because the rapids will become grade II and then abruptly go quiet 50 yards before the crown of Alexian Falls. Portaging around Alexian Falls is recommended, as the Red River squeezes through a tight narrows perhaps five feet wide, and then drops 20 feet as it flows through a 40-foot-long chute. There is a giant chunk of granite right in the middle of the falls that can cause serious problems for your canoe or kayak (and whoever is in the canoe or kayak).

A mile downstream from Alexian Falls the river again narrows and splits into two, eight-foot-wide channels that become the grade II spillway known as Ziemers Falls. The drop is only a few feet but paddlers should scout Ziemers before attacking either channel. You will want to pause along the river for a few photos and lunch before taking out at County Hwy A, 1.5 miles downstream from Ziemers Falls.

Directions: Both waterfalls are surrounded by private property, but they can be reached by canoe or kayak from below the Gresham power dam 1.3 miles east of the city to a take-out point four miles downstream where County Hwy A crosses the river in the Town of Red River.

Canada geese

Chapter 7
SAUK COUNTY

My ears became attuned to the soft burble of Parfrey's Creek as I walked slowly up the snow-covered path. I imagined Robert Parfrey, the Englishman who purchased this property in 1865, watching the water cascade down the long flume, built on a wooden trestle, that brought the creek water from a mud and log impoundment on Parfrey's Creek to Robert's grist mill.

In the narrow sandstone chasm of Parfrey's Glen footbridges spanned the creek in several places as the path wound its way up through the ravine, snaking along in the perfect calm of a mid-February morning. I came to a sign dedicated to Norman Carter Fassett, who was responsible for naming Parfrey's Glen the state's first Natural Area. I walked beneath mammoth stone outcroppings. Yellow birch clung to the sheer walls of the gorge, their roots embedded in the scant soil, seeming to defy gravity as they leaned out and over the creek bed.

Huge boulders that had fallen from the 100-foot-high walls lay on the canyon floor, Parfrey's Creek weaving among them. I was the first person to enter since the recent snowfall. However, the fresh tracks of a vole showed where it popped out of a snowbank, scampered 25 yards on top of the snow, and then disappeared into a neat, round hole where it was undoubtedly hiding at that very moment. The canyon became brighter then, and I knew I was nearing the north end and Parfrey's Glen Waterfall.

The gorge ended, opening up to the woods at the north end. The left wall of the gorge was perhaps 50 feet high and completely covered with a quilt of turquoise-blue ice. Fat icicles hung from the cliff, their tips dripping slightly from the midday warmth of the sun. I lifted my camera to capture the enchanting scene.

(Left) *Parfrey's Glen Waterfall*

Parfrey's Glen Creek, Sauk County

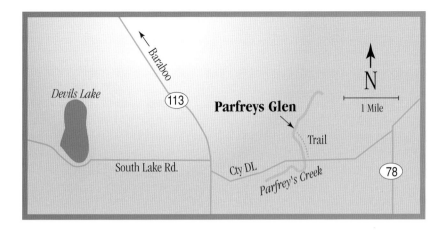

Parfrey's Glen Waterfall

Location: Parfrey's Glen Creek, seven miles southeast of Baraboo.

Directions: From Baraboo, take State Hwy 113 south approximately five miles to County Hwy DL. Go east on Hwy DL. There is no sign for Parfrey's Glen here, but there is a sign just prior to the intersection that reads "Devil's Head Resort, 2 miles." Follow County Hwy DL 1.9 miles and watch for the parking lot on the north (left) side of the road and a sign for Parfrey's Glen. A state park sticker is required at Parfrey's Glen; if a ranger is not on duty there is a self-pay station.

Ever since first owner and namesake Robert Parfrey left here and moved to Minnesota in 1876, curious sightseers have flocked to this gorgeous little glen to picnic and to hike into the canyon to see the layers of sandstone and quartzite formations and Parfrey's Glen Waterfall. Access is now limited to one trail to protect the unusual plants in the glen.

The half-mile-long trail begins at the parking lot and continues through the woods up a gradual hill. In summer you'll see the interesting and fragile plant community in the glen. A bamboo-like plant called scouring-rush, for example, is a rare species that researchers have studied here for many years. It derives its name from the fact that pioneers were able to scour their pots and pans with it due to silica in the stems. Other endangered or rare plants and trees in Parfrey's Glen include mountain maple, red elder, clintonia, and mountain clubmoss.

The trail soon narrows and the terrain becomes steeper. Hickory, white oak, and mountain maples sprout from the stony earth. You cross and re-cross Parfrey's Creek on several bridges as the trail climbs higher into the Baraboo Hills. The path goes past outcroppings of sandstone and crosses another bridge. Sunlight dims as the towering 100-foot-high walls, rimmed with tenacious trees, hide the sun. In fact, the flora in the gorge resembles that of northern Wisconsin because of the way the air settles in the bottom of the canyon and to the way sunlight is limited by the overhanging rock and the leafy canopy.

At the end of the trail a railed viewing area faces Parfrey's Glen Waterfall, which flows over a six-foot drop 30 yards in front of you. The falls are at the end of the canyon, and the creek flows through the woods, over the waterfall, and into the gorge.

High Falls, Baptism River

Chapter 8
MINNESOTA

From the waterfalls in Amnicon and Pattison state parks in Douglas County, Wisconsin, it's a short drive to some of Minnesota's most beautiful cascades. Duluth, which is built on a steep hillside facing Lake Superior, is home to Lester Falls on the Lester River and Amity Falls on Amity Creek. Both these waterfalls are in Lester Park on the northeast side of the city and can be reached by a short walk.

Another great place to enjoy wonderful rapids and waterfalls is at Jay Cooke State Park. A 20-minute drive from South Duluth, Jay Cooke State Park features several waterfalls on the St. Louis River.

Of course, no venture to waterfalls in Minnesota would be complete without a drive up the rocky and wild Lake Superior North Shore through parts of St. Louis and Lake counties.

An hour north of Duluth is Gooseberry Falls State Park, with its five awesome waterfalls. Waterfalls like Lester, Amity, and Gooseberry are within a 90-minute drive of Wisconsin. They are located in Lake, St. Louis, or Hennepin counties and none are south of Minneapolis.

Lower Falls, Gooseberry River, north shore Lake Superior

LAKE COUNTY, MINNESOTA
Gooseberry Falls

Location: Gooseberry River, north shore Lake Superior, 12 miles northeast of Two Harbors, Silver Creek Township.

Directions: Take U.S. Hwy 61 north from Duluth through Two Harbors to Gooseberry Falls State Park. The drive is a little over an hour. A park entry permit is required. (See map p.97)

Five superb waterfalls decorate this gorgeous 1600-acre state park on the shore of Lake Superior. Visitors flock to Gooseberry Falls to see the spectacular waterfalls along the Gooseberry River as it darts down the Nester Bluffs on its way to Lake Superior.

The most popular waterfalls are the Upper and Lower falls, as these are closest to the highway with parking readily available (except summer weekends and holidays when it pays to get there as early as possible). Both waterfalls can be seen from the bridge on Hwy 61, but traffic flow does not allow even a quick view. The trails to both falls are short and well worn.

Upper Falls plunges 30 feet into a swirling pool. Below Upper Falls, the river turns and flows south under the Hwy 61 bridge, widens across a bed of hardened lava, and then descends in two stages over the top of Lower Falls. The first stage is a 25-foot drop onto a 60-foot-long ledge, from which the falls plunges another 40 feet in its second stage.

I prefer Fifth Falls, however, not only because it is less crowded most days, but because the half-hour hike to the falls is invigorating and beautiful. Whether stepping along the hardpan of the Superior Hiking Trail or leaping across the occasional mudpuddle on the Fifth Falls Trail, the walk to Fifth Falls always holds a surprise—a pileated woodpecker rapping on an ancient white pine tree, a raccoon waddling through a grove of quaking aspen and paper birch, its belly distended from a hardy meal of thimbleberries, or perhaps a glimpse of lavender mertensia, Canada mayflowers, wintergreen, asters, and other wildflowers that adorn the trail.

At Fifth Falls the river drops 35 feet over chunks of lava and into a narrow gorge. The walls of red and black rock are pocked with oblong caves and caverns, etched from the steady onslaught of water and sand from the stream above. Spruce and hemlock grow from the grassy ledges. Water trickles from cracks and crevasses. A fine mist keeps the rocks wet, and a bright sun can create a rainbow over the gorge.

Along the trail to Fifth Falls you'll pass two smaller, unnamed waterfalls with drops of about 10 feet each—small potatoes in this area, but beautiful nonetheless.

(Right) Lower Falls

High Falls, Baptism River

LAKE COUNTY
High Falls

Location: Baptism River, 4.5 miles north of Silver Bay, Tettegouche State Park, Beaver Bay Township.

Directions: From Duluth take U.S. Hwy 61 along the north shore of Lake Superior for approximately 58 miles to Tettegouche State Park. A park entry permit is required.

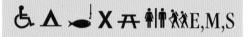

Tettegouche State Park contains an outstanding combination of natural features, vegetation and wildlife, as well as three gorgeous waterfalls. The park has 17 miles of hiking trails, which are the only way to get to its five lakes and to its primitive camping and picnic facilities.

Two of the three waterfalls along the Baptism River are easily accessible on a trail leading from the park's main entrance. The first falls, though closest to the entrance, is off the beaten path. It is called The Cascades and with its gradual 12-foot descent is the smallest of the three. It's a grade III-IV rapids from spring through mid-summer. The next falls upstream is unnamed.

The third waterfall is High Falls, a thundering 80-foot beauty that crashes into a deep gorge. A swinging steel suspension bridge along the Superior Hiking Trail crosses the Baptism River just upstream from High Falls, allowing hikers to reach the waterfall from the east bank to see the falls from a different perspective.

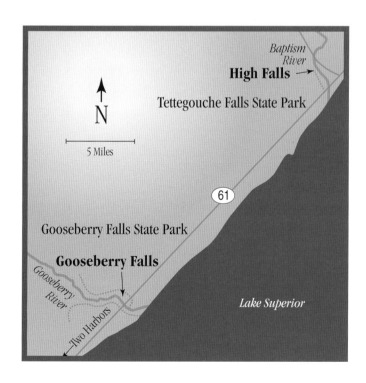

Amity Falls, Amity Creek

ST. LOUIS COUNTY
Amity Falls
Lester Falls

Location: Both of these waterfalls are located in Lester Park, Duluth.

Directions: Take U.S. Hwy 61 east through Duluth to 61st Avenue East. Turn left (north) and stay on 61st Avenue three blocks until you reach the parking lot at Lester Park. This is the simplest route. However, as you travel east on Hwy 61 through Duluth you will see a sign at 45th Avenue directing you north to Lester Park. Beyond that sign there are no more directions to Lester Park. If you turn on 45th Avenue, go five blocks to East Superior Street, turn east (right), and then follow it to 61st Avenue East, which is also known as Lester River Road. Turn left and go a half block to the parking area.

Lester Park is shaped roughly like a slice of pie bounded by Amity Creek and the Lester River, which join just below the Superior Street Bridge.

Leaving the car in the parking lot, take the fieldstone bridge that crosses the Lester River and follow the gravel path on the other side, passing a playground and several picnic tables on your left and a shelter house on your right. After you reach Amity Creek you can either walk south to where it joins the Lester River, or you can take the path north and follow Amity Creek 400 yards through a cedar forest to the top of Amity Falls.

Amity Falls can also be reached on Occidental Road a block west of Lester River Road. Take Occidental Road 0.5 mile north and watch for the stone bridge that spans the falls. A wooden sign attached to the bridge says "Lester Park."

Amity Falls tumbles 40 feet over a rocky face at a point where Amity Creek takes a sharp, 90-degree turn from northwest to south. Below the falls the creek flows between basalt buttresses as it is forced through the narrow gorge to its meeting with the Lester River.

A 0.3-mile hike north from the parking area along the Lester River will take you to Lester Falls, which is 50 feet high and more impressive than Amity Falls. You will notice immediately that the boulders in the Lester River dwarf those in Amity Creek and that the river is wider and faster than its sister on the west side of the park. Lester Falls can also be partially seen from a vehicle from the east on Lester River Road.

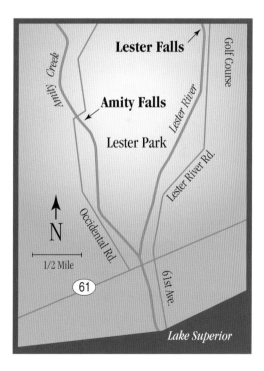

Lester Falls, Lester River

CARLTON COUNTY
Swinging Bridge Falls

Location: St. Louis River, three miles east of Carlton and 10 miles southwest of Duluth, Jay Cooke State Park.

Directions: Go east from Carlton on State Hwy 210 to Jay Cooke State Park. From Duluth take U.S. Hwy 2 west to the State Hwy 23 (Grand Avenue) exit and follow it through Smithville, New Duluth, and Fond du Lac where Hwy 23 meets Hwy 210 at a fork. Take Hwy 210 (the right hand fork) 6.2 miles to the park. Swinging Bridge Falls is located behind the headquarters building on the St. Louis River. A park entry permit is required.

 ♿ ⛺ 🎣 ✕ 🪑 🚻 🥾 E,M,S

In Jay Cooke State Park the St. Louis River is a torrent of rapids and outcroppings that create dozens of waterfalls, large and small. The largest waterfall, a 12-footer that glows golden in the late afternoon sun, is Swinging Bridge Falls.

The swinging bridge is a suspension bridge constructed across the river behind the park headquarters building. To give you an idea of the ferocity of the spring runoff, this bridge was once demolished during spring high water. The water-fall can be seen from the bridge, from the shore next to the bridge, or from the shore on the opposite side after hiking a short trail.

The geology of the St. Louis River here is quite remarkable. Much of the bedrock is exposed, especially when the spring floods sub-side. Eons ago, thick mud deposits were tightly compacted and formed shale. Over time, the shale was transformed into slate by movement of the earth, pressure, and intense heat. As the earth's crust moved, the slate beds began to fold and crack; today the sheets of rock lean at an angle. As the St. Louis nears Lake Superior, the slate formations disappear under the red clay that covers the bedrock.

Swinging Bridge Falls, St. Louis River

Minnehaha Falls

Location: Minnehaha Creek, Minnehaha Parkway, southeast side of Minneapolis.

Directions: Several main highways run near Minnehaha City Park where the waterfall is located. Just north of the International Airport, State Hwy 55 crosses Minnehaha Creek. Several ramps off Hwy 55 here will connect you with Minnehaha Parkway and the park. The exit at 42nd Avenue South is the easiest.

Minnehaha Creek runs through one of the nation's busiest metropolitan areas. Fifty-foot-high Minnehaha Falls has survived all the urban growth around it untouched, nestled in a lovely green oasis. The canyon through which Minnehaha Creek flows over the falls is composed of compressed layers of sandstone and limestone. A half mile downstream from the falls, the creek joins the Mississippi River.

The large park contains an interpretive center with historical information about the pioneers and Indians who lived here.

(Left and right) *Minnehaha Falls*

Chapter 9

MICHIGAN

As one can imagine, the same rocky escarpment under northern Wisconsin continues eastward into Michigan, where the Gogebic Range is home to many creeks and rivers, and, consequently, rapids and waterfalls. An excursion from Black River Harbor and Rainbow Falls, following a scenic section of the North Country Trail as it skirts County Road 513 on the west side of the Black River, past Sandstone, Gorge, Potawatomi, and other superb waterfalls, will satisfy the most discriminating waterfall hunter, and provide a beautiful day in the woods as well.

This chapter is devoted to waterfalls that can be found within a short drive of the Wisconsin-Michigan border. All the Michigan waterfalls in this chapter are in Gogebic County in the far northwestern part of Michigan's Upper Peninsula. Some other Michigan waterfalls are actually on the Michigan-Wisconsin border and are therefore described in the Wisconsin chapters of this book.

(Left) *Rainbow Falls, Black River*

(above) *Sandstone Falls, Black River*

GOGEBIC COUNTY
Rainbow Falls

Location: Black River, 13.5 miles north of Bessemer.

> **Directions:** Head west on U.S. Hwy 2 from Bessemer and watch for the County Road (CR) 513 turn-off to the north. Take CR 513 to Black River Harbor on Lake Superior, where there's ample parking. Follow the trail signs from the parking lot, over the suspension bridge on the Black River, and into the conifer forest. Stay on the Rainbow Falls hiking trail approximately 0.75 mile and listen for the falls. This trail is strenuous in sections, particularly at the beginning.
>
> Rainbow Falls can also be reached from the first parking area 0.5 mile south of Black River Harbor going south toward Bessemer on CR 513. A "Rainbow Falls" sign will direct you eastward into the parking area. The trail to the falls here is shorter than from Black River Harbor, but is also difficult. It is nearly all downhill on both a trail and almost 200 wooden steps that take you to an observation platform that provides a perfect view of the Black River and Rainbow Falls.
>
>

Rainbow Falls is closest to Lake Superior in a series of eight waterfalls along Michigan's Black River north of the town of Bessemer. Rainbow Falls is the most spectacular and the most beauti-ful of the eight. From the parking lot on CR 513, you descend 200 wooden steps down a steep, thickly forested embankment to the viewing platform that puts you above the crown of Rainbow Falls. Going down is the easy part. It is the slow, methodical climbing up the steps afterward that encourages visitors to prolong their stay at Rainbow, a sort of natural way to capture an audience so they come to fully appreciate the rare beauty of the waterfall.

Getting to Rainbow Falls from Black River Harbor on the shore of Lake Superior is not only a longer walk, it is a more invigorating hike on a lightly used trail. You end up directly across the waterfall from the viewing platform reached by the trail from CR 513. On this trail, wooden steps traverse the knobby outcropping at the harbor. Then the trail ascends into a magnificent conifer forest, past lookouts that offer an incredible view of Lake Superior.

Across a weathered footbridge you go, then around a bend dappled with fern and wood violets, up a ridge and down an embankment, and then you see the river below and hear the thunder of the falls. Rainbow Falls is actually two waterfalls. The one on the right side crashes 45 feet straight down into a dark pool. The left-hand falls is a narrower and more forceful cataract that gushes between two huge chunks of rock and snakes right and then left as it plunges into the basin underneath a protective cloak of mist.

On a bright day when the angle of the sun hits the falls just right, you will be treated to the phenomenon for which this waterfall is named. Watch for the rainbow to appear against the cliff on the east side of the falls.

Mallard hen and ducklings

GOGEBIC COUNTY
Sandstone Falls

Location: Black River, 13 miles north of Bessemer.

Directions: From the Rainbow Falls parking area (see previous entry) go south on County Road (CR) 513 about 0.5 mile to the Sandstone Falls parking lot on the left side of the road. The trail begins there.

M,S

The hike to beautiful Sandstone Falls is only 0.25 mile but the final descent is steep and may be difficult for some, especially on the way back out to the car.

As the name implies, the riverbed here is smooth, hard sandstone that has eroded over the eons. Sandstone Falls has two pitches. The first is a five-foot drop onto a sandstone ledge. From there the river plunges 20 feet into a dark pool. Then it flows downstream to Rainbow Falls.

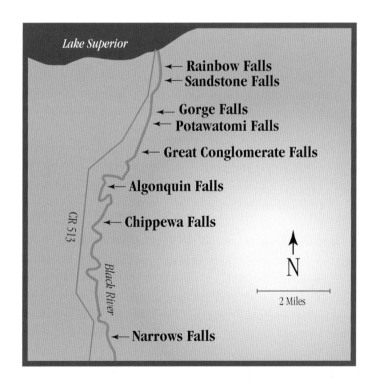

Gorge Falls, Black River

GOGEBIC COUNTY
Gorge Falls
Potawatomi Falls

Location: Black River, 12 miles north of Bessemer.

Directions: From the Sandstone Falls parking area (see previous entry) go south and watch for the large sign on the right directing you into the Potawatomi and Gorge falls turnout on the east side of CR 513, approximately one mile south of the Sandstone Falls parking area. The U.S. Forest Service does an outstanding job marking all the waterfalls along CR 513. The parking lot is located a few hundred feet off CR 513. The trails for Potawatomi Falls and Gorge Falls begin at the parking lot.

The walk into Gorge Falls is easy and takes only a couple of minutes. The path is wide and firm, and soon you reach a T intersection. To the right, or south, is the way to Potawatomi Falls; the left trail leads to Gorge Falls. Take the left trail and follow the railings along the cliff an eighth of a mile to a series of steps and decks that take you down to the platform overlooking the Black River and Gorge Falls.

The Black River here squeezes through an eight-foot narrows before it drops 20 feet to the bottom of the gorge. The waterfall looks like a long, smooth water slide, and for a moment you wonder what it would be like to take the plunge on a hot summer's day!

Downstream in the direction of Lake Superior, clutching the towering walls of the Black River gorge, wildflowers and trees seem to defy gravity as they cling to the thin topsoil along the craggy bluffs. The river meanders from here downstream to Sandstone Falls.

In winter the river gorge is absolutely enchanting! Big globs of snow cling to the branches of cedars and hemlock. Ice chunks drop across Gorge Falls and break into a hundred pieces near the edges of the pool beneath. Everything is white and peaceful, except the rushing water. Winter visitors can hike into the falls on snowshoes.

The walk to Potawatomi Falls (to the right where the trails to the two falls split) follows the river gorge to a short series of wooden steps that take you to Potawatomi Falls.

Potawatomi Falls is about 40 feet high, and is split into two uneven halves. On the near (west) side of the river the waterfall flows around a bulge in the underlying rock. The falls on the east side of the river are wider and smoother. At the bottom, the two flows join and move downstream toward Gorge Falls.

The viewing area at Potawatomi Falls is a giant outcropping of sandstone on the west side of the gorge. It is not protected by railings. Be careful here, especially if you have kids with you. After contemplating Potawatomi Falls and Gorge Falls, take time for a picnic at one of the picnic areas near the trailhead.

GOGEBIC COUNTY
Great Conglomerate Falls

Location: Black River, 11 miles north of Bessemer.

Directions: The parking area for Great Conglomerate Falls is located about a mile south of the Gorge Falls parking area along County Road 513 toward Bessemer. It is clearly marked. (See map p.107)

🚶🚶M,S

Great Conglomerate Falls

Signs at the Great Conglomerate Falls parking area explain the geology of the Black River basin and its marvelous waterfalls. The 0.75-mile trail begins at the parking lot and immediately descends into the conifer forest. The first part is a gentle slope, almost unnoticeable, but you soon begin a steeper decline. The final segment near the waterfall is steep, but there are wooden stairs and railings along the way. Along the trail are benches cut from local deadfalls if you need to take a breather.

Great Conglomerate takes its name from the mammoth conglomerate rock deposited here in the Black River. The waterfall splits into two halves, then drops 35 feet in three steps. The river churns at the bottom of the falls, gathers new momentum, and continues its flow downstream to Potawatomi Falls. Below the falls the canyon walls on both sides of the river are over 100 feet high.

(Left) *Potawatomi Falls, Black River*

Great Conglomerate Falls, Black River

GOGEBIC COUNTY
Algonquin Falls

Location: Black River, 9.5 miles north of Bessemer.

Directions: From Bessemer take County Road (CR) 513 north about nine miles to the turn-off for the Copper Peak Ski Flying Hill. Stay on CR 513 past the fork in the road and continue approximately 0.75 mile to where the roads rejoin on the back side of Copper Peak. At that intersection make a sharp right turn toward the ski jump and go 0.2 mile. There you will see a sign marking the trailhead for the North Country Trail. Park on either side of the road and follow the North Country Trail to the north (left—that's the only direction the trail goes). Algonquin Falls is approximately 0.5 mile, Great Conglomerate Falls is three miles, Potawatomi and Gorge falls are 3.5 miles, and Rainbow Falls is five miles up the trail from that point. (See map p.107)

Algonquin Falls gradually drops six feet over a rocky 50-yard stretch of river. It's a grade III rapids in spring and grade II the rest of the year. The best thing about the hike into Algonquin Falls along the North Country Trail is the breathtaking beauty of the river, the forest, and the wildlife in this gorgeous area deep in the Ottawa National Forest. I recommend spending an entire day to hike the North Country Trail along the Black River to view the six waterfalls.

Hike to Algonquin Falls, then continue all the way north to Rainbow Falls, stopping to see Great Conglomerate, Potawatomi, Gorge, and Sandstone falls along the way. This journey will take about three hours depending on your speed and how often you stop to fish or take pictures. Carry plenty of drinking water, food, and bug spray. From Rainbow Falls you can hike another half mile to Black River Harbor on Lake Superior. When you reach Rainbow Falls, or Lake Superior, take a break and then return to your car by walking south down CR 513 to the parking area. The walk along CR 513 will take 90 minutes or more, but it is mostly downhill. At day's end you will have done some serious exercising, and you will have seen some of Michigan's most phenomenal scenery.

Chippewa Falls, Black River

GOGEBIC COUNTY
Chippewa Falls

Location: Black River, 8.5 miles north of Bessemer.

Directions: From Bessemer go north on County Road (CR) 513 eight miles to the sign on the right-hand side directing you to the Copper Peak Ski Flying Hill. Turn right (east) into the Copper Peak area and drive about 0.5 mile to the gift shop below the ski jumping hill. Just past the shop is a dirt road that leads south across a field where the ski flyers land. Park at the end of the field and walk directly south from the end of the landing zone a quarter mile to the river. (See map p.107)

The descent to Chippewa Falls is rough and steep, through dense underbrush with large, loose rocks scattered on the hillside, making walking difficult. There is no marked trail to Chippewa Falls, although you'll hear the Black River. Follow the sound to locate the falls. Read your compass before you descend into the canyon, and note the back-azimuth (reciprocal reading) for the trek out. You will reach the Black River in five to ten minutes.

The river is about 100 feet wide above the falls and is dotted with hundreds of large boulders scattered in the riverbed. Chippewa Falls, which is a grade II and III rapids during high water, drops 10 feet in two stages. Below the falls the river carves a deep cut into the right-hand bank as it makes a sharp turn.

Take your time on the hike up the ravine to the top of the hill. Wear gloves so you can grab stems and branches. In daylight you should be able to see the ski jump on top of Copper Peak; at night, use your compass to find your way.

GOGEBIC COUNTY
Narrows Falls

Location: Black River, 5.5 miles north of Bessemer.

Directions: Go 6.8 miles north on County Road (CR) 513 from Bessemer and watch for the sign on your right (east) announcing the Narrows Spring Campground. Leave your vehicle in the parking area and walk through the park. (See map p.107)

The Black River flows quietly by the campground a few feet down the hill on the east side of the park. Take the old wooden steps down the muddy embankment. The walk to the river is short and easy, but coming back is uphill all the way and a bit more strenuous.

Narrows Falls is just below where Narrows Creek meets the Black River. Early in the year the falls are quite turbulent, but as spring extends into summer, the depth of the river drops enough to make the waterfall a grade II rapids. The site is pretty any time of the year; a snowshoe adventure is a perfect way to check out the wilderness here. Trout fishing is excellent below the falls. The river is amazingly deep on the inside corners of its banks, which is where brook and German brown trout hide.

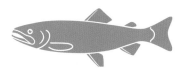

GOGEBIC COUNTY
Neepikon Falls

Location: Black River, 1.5 miles north of Ramsay.

Most of the year Neepikon Falls is a grade II rapids that drops 10 feet over a 100-yard stretch of river as it flows through a deep canyon. Early spring is the best time to view these cascades. This will involve trudging through snow depths of up to three feet, so bring your snowshoes. When the snows have melted the hike through the clearing is easy. However, once the clearing ends, you will have to poke your way through thick brush and a dense tangle of limbs. Take your time here and enjoy the variety of ground cover plants such as wild strawberry and heartleaf arnica that dot the soggy ground. Watch for white-tailed deer on the edge of the clearing and river otters near the shore.

Directions: Approximately two miles west of Wakefield on U.S. Hwy 2 look for Blackjack Road and the "Blackjack Ski Resort" sign on the north side of the highway. Turn north on Blackjack Road and follow it 0.8 mile to the Northern Natural Gas Company pumping station on the east (right) side of the road. Park off to the side and walk west 0.25 mile down the clearing you see across the road. Within a few yards of the river the clearing abruptly ends and you must make your own path through the pine trees and brush. Neepikon Falls is located about 250 yards upstream from where the pipeline crosses the river.

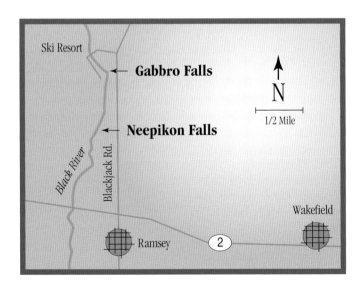

Gabbro Falls, Black River

GOGEBIC COUNTY
Gabbro Falls

Location: Black River, two miles north of Ramsay.

The twin cascades of Gabbro Falls make for one of the most impressive and dramatic waterfalls in the Midwest. The falls on the east side of the river drop an unimpeded 60 feet into the pool below. Below the falls a fine mist rises almost to the top of the cascade, partially blocking the falls from view.

Approach the west bank carefully; there is no barricade. On this side of the river the flow has been narrowed to only a few feet, creating a most extraordinary burst of water. This half of Gabbro Falls drops 10 feet into a swirling pool and then down another 40 feet, bouncing off tree trunks and anything else that has become lodged in the rocks during spring runoff. After this dramatic drop, the flow turns 90 degrees, plummets an additional 10 feet, and then meets the water from its twin.

Directions: Approximately two miles west of Wakefield on U.S. Hwy 2 look for Blackjack Road and the "Blackjack Ski Resort" sign on the north side of the highway. Turn north on Blackjack Road and follow it 1.3 miles to an open strip of land with a set of power lines running its length. Park off to the side and walk this strip 0.25 mile to the Black River, then turn north and follow your ears to the falls 100 yards downstream.

To reach the other side of Gabbro Falls continue on Blackjack Road through a sharp curve to the left, cross the Black River, pass through the covered bridge entering the ski resort, and then follow the road to your left as it climbs a hill. Halfway up on the right side you will see a small building where you can make a U turn to park facing downhill. The short trail begins here. (See map p.116)

GOGEBIC COUNTY
Powder Horn Falls

Location: Powder Mill Creek, two miles northwest of Bessemer.

Directions: Just west of Bessemer on U.S. Hwy 2 is a large sign on the north side of the road advertising the Powder Horn Ski Resort. This is Powder Horn Road. Follow it 1.75 miles and watch for the Powder Mill Inn on the right. At the second power pole south of the Inn, on the same side of the road, is the trailhead for the falls. There is room for three vehicles to park. The waterfall is only a couple hundred yards away on a well-used path.

Arranged tightly between two rocky columns that stand 75 feet high, Powder Mill Creek narrows to three feet in width and drops 12 feet over smooth rock. The creek widens again as it is carried over the main falls that plunge another 40 feet. A fine mist rises from the river, providing life-giving nourishment to the wonderful assortment of ferns, flowers, and vines that flourish in the ravine.

The view from the base of Powder Horn Falls is amazing. Reaching it is a bit tricky—down a steep bank of loose granite—but if you take your time and are careful you will see where a usable trail has been established. Downstream from the falls, Powder Mill Creek turns 90 degrees to the north, flows around a small island, and continues its journey to the Black River 0.5 mile downstream

Powder Horn Falls, Powder Mill Creek

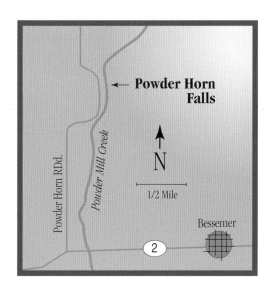

Chapter 10
PHOTOGRAPHING WATERFALLS AND CALCULATING THEIR FLOW

PHOTOGRAPHY

There are two key challenges in waterfall photography. The first is that most waterfalls are often in shadow during the time of day that is most important to photographers, early morning and late afternoon. I can think of several Wisconsin waterfalls that face east or west that are still in shadow because of overhanging trees even when the sun is shining on them.

The other problem photographing waterfalls is our seasonally gray skies. During periods of highest flow in spring, just when waterfall watching is at its peak, sunshine is at a premium, providing another challenge to the photographer. Sunny days in winter are also rare, but I do not let that influence my plans to snowshoe into ice-covered waterfalls for a day of taking photos. I adapt to gray skies in winter and spring by using faster-speed films, longer exposure times, using my telephoto lens to "crop" the picture to limit the sky in many photos, and using black and white film.

Early morning is my favorite time to photograph a waterfall. Light is softer at this time of day, resulting in beautiful images of subjects I might include with the waterfall: birds, plants clinging to the cliff, a length of tree jammed against the face of the falls. Another reason to get to the river early is that you'll probably be the only person there, which means you won't have to wait for people to get out of the way of your perfect shot.

Late afternoon is the other best time to photograph waterfalls. The light then is often as good as that in early morning, especially if you can capture the last glow of sunlight. However, you may encounter more people enjoying the falls at twilight.

I will photograph during midday, the period between 10 a.m. and 2 p.m., but I use a polarizing filter with slide film on a bright day or a yellow, orange, or red filter if I'm using black and white film (depending on the clouds and the amount of blue sky).

I use a Nikon 90S camera body, which allows manual or auto focusing, shutter speeds up to 1/8000 second, and a wide range of apertures. It has auto film advance, and a time delay feature. For most waterfall shots I use either a 35-70mm f/3.3 or a 70-210mm f/4 Nikor zoom lens. I use a 90mm f/4 macro for scenic and close-up shots.

I suggest you choose one or two types of film and use them consistently. For color slides I use Kodachrome 64 and 25, and Fujichrome Velvia with an ISO (ASA) of 50. Most of the images in this book were shot with Kodachrome 64 slide film. For black and white images I use Kodak TMAX film in either 100 or 400 speed depending on available light and motion of the waterfall.

Where lighting is marginal, or when shooting with long exposure times (1/60 of a second or slower), you will need a tripod. My camera kit includes a Bogen 3021 tripod with a Bogen 3047 head. This combination is flexible and light enough (about seven pounds) to carry easily.

(Left) *Morgan Falls, South Branch, Morgan Creek, Wisconsin*

Swinging Bridge Falls, St. Louis River, Minnesota

You can take great photographs of waterfalls at dusk or twilight by using available moonlight or by reflecting light from a campfire toward the waterfall. However, illuminating a waterfall with an artificial light source such as headlights or flashlight beam, or by using a flash mechanism on your camera, washes out the details of the falls.

It takes awhile to become a good waterfall photographer. Experiment with shutter speeds and aperture settings and don't hesitate to override your camera's automatic features to operate it manually. Don't rely totally on your camera's built-in exposure meter. Learn how to use a hand-held exposure meter. Take photos from a variety of locations and angles. Stand at the top and shoot straight down the cascade. Wade into the shallower pools below waterfalls and aim your camera directly up toward the top. Slide in behind a waterfall and shoot through the flow. (Be sure to protect your camera from the spray.) The best part about waterfall photography is that taking the time to size up a waterfall and decide how best to photograph it gives you the time to study and appreciate all its attributes. This alone makes photographing waterfalls worthwhile.

CALCULATING THE FLOW
OVER A WATERFALL   *by Tom Lisi*

My dad gets a lot of questions about whether or not there is a way to tell how much water is flowing over a waterfall. I'm an engineer, so he asked me to come up with a relatively easy way to measure the flow.

The flow rate for a waterfall can be expressed in gallons of water per second. You can measure the flow either just upstream or just downstream from the waterfall. Look for a spot where flow conditions are fairly constant, that is, the width, depth, and speed of flow are the same for a short distance so you can take some measurements. (See Figure 1). Don't worry if your test section isn't the same size, shape, or speed as the waterfall itself because the amount of flow will be the same in the river as the flow going over the falls. After all, where would the water go if not over the falls?

The information you need for the calculations in the test section of river is as follows:

A= Cross sectional area of the river,
    in square feet
D=Average depth of the river, in feet
W=Width of the river, in feet
V=Average stream speed, in feet per second
L=Length of the test section, in feet
T=Test time, in seconds

Knowing the speed and the cross sectional area will allow us to calculate:

Q=Flow rate of the river, in gallons per second

To visualize the cross sectional area, imagine a fish's view of the river, facing upstream (see Figure 2). This is a bit simplified, but it is the shape of an average riverbed. You'll have to estimate the width, and probably the depth, too, unless you have some equipment such as a long tape measure (and a way to get to the other side) and a weight tied to a string (and a convenient bridge from which to lower the weight into the water). Using the average riverbed diagram, after you estimate or measure the width and depth, use this equation to get the cross sectional area:

$$A = (W/4) \times D + (W/2) \times D$$

Average stream velocity (V) is the distance an object floating in the middle of the stream travels in a given time period. Throw in a stick and time it as it floats through your test section. Use the equation V=L/T (that's Length divided by Time).

Now that we have calculated the velocity and the cross sectional area of the river, we can calculate the flow using this equation:

$$Q = V \times A \times 7.48$$

(7.48 converts the answer, which is in cubic feet per second, to gallons per second. If you want the flow in cubic feet per second, don't multiply by 7.48.)

Now that you understand the equations, here are a few hints to help with the calculations.

1. Bring note paper, a calculator, a stopwatch (or a least a watch with a second hand), a 100-foot tape measure, and a weight that's at least a half pound, preferably more, attached to a strong length of twine or heavy string.

2. For your test section of river, you'll need a stretch that's anywhere from 20 feet to 200 feet

long, with enough of a path alongside it that you can follow your floating object. If there's a bridge where you're taking these measurements, use the river directly downstream—taking the measurements will be easier, safer, and more accurate.

3. When you measure velocity, be sure that whatever you use is large enough to be easily watched as it bounces along on the waves. I've found that a piece of wood that's about two inches by six inches is large enough. For math reasons, it's easiest to do the velocity test for a number of seconds that is easily divisible, regardless of the length the floating object travels. I like to use 10, 20, or 100 seconds. For example, if your piece of wood traveled 70 feet in 10 seconds, the velocity would be V=70/10 = 7 feet per second. If you have a calculator, though, it may be easier to measure a set distance on the bank and see how long it takes your piece of wood to travel that distance. Having a friend at the other end to record time also helps, as some rivers flow faster than you can walk. Throw the wood or other object into the middle of the stream. Start timing when it hits the water. Calculate the velocity three times and use the average of the three values.

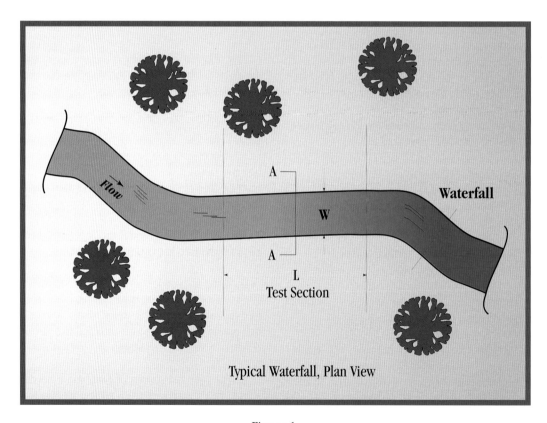

Figure 1

4. If you're not good at estimating distance, you can pace off a certain distance, using one pace as approximately three feet. Using that as a reference, estimate the width. If you're lucky enough to have a bridge, use your tape measure, or pace the distance between the banks on the bridge.

5. It's very difficult to estimate depth, so it's best to measure it if you can (but be very careful if you wade out into a rushing river to do this—don't try wading if the water is more than knee-deep). Again, it's best if you can dangle the weight from a bridge and then measure the length of wet string. Measure the depth in the middle of the river if possible.

And remember, these calculations will give you only a rough approximation. It requires sophisticated instruments to measure the flow down to the last gallon per second. But then, the measurement of your experience as you enjoy the river and the waterfall won't depend on how many gallons per minute are roaring over the falls.

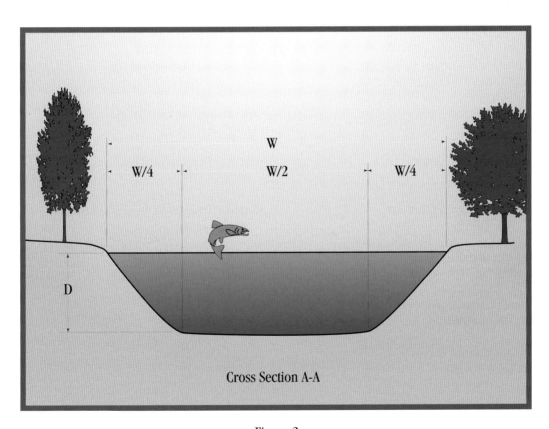

Cross Section A-A

Figure 2

FOR MORE INFORMATION
AND TO CHECK ON CURRENT CONDITIONS

Wisconsin Dept of Tourism
800 372-2737 or 608 266-2161

Douglas County Chamber of Commerce
715 394-7716

Pattison State Park
715 399-8073

Amnicon Falls State Park
715 398-3000

Bayfield County Chamber of Commerce
715 373-3335

Ashland Area Chamber of Commerce
800-284-9484 or 715-682-2500

Copper Falls State Park
715 274-5123

US Forest Service Glidden
715 264-2511

Hurley Chamber of Commerce
715 561-4334

Osceola Business Association
715 755-3300

Sawyer County Chamber of Commerce
715 634-8662

Phillips Chamber of Commerce
715 339-4100

Eau Claire Chamber of Commerce
715 834-1204

DNR Regional Office, Eau Claire
715 839-3700

Wausau Chamber of Commerce
715 845-6231

Nicolet National Forest, Rhinelander
715 362-1306

Marinette County Chamber of Commerce
715 735-6681

Menominee Indian Reservation, Keshena
715 799-3341

DNR Regional Office, Green Bay
920 492-5800

Sauk County Chamber of Commerce
608 356-8333

Minnesota Department of Tourism
800 657-3700

Minnesota Department of Natural Resources
800 766-6000

Gooseberry Falls State Park
218 834-3855

Tettegouche State Park
218 266-3539

Jay Cooke State Park
218 384-4610

Michigan Department of Tourism
906 663-4542

Saxon Falls, Montreal River

ABOUT THE AUTHOR

Pat Lisi is a Wisconsin conservation warden. He has been a freelance writer and editor of several newsletters and in-house magazines. He has been an outdoor photographer for more than 25 years. He published a novel, *My Time in Hell*, in 1975, and in 1991 he published the first edition of *A Guide to Wisconsin's Waterfalls*. Pat's wife, Marjorie, was responsible for the maps in this book and is the computer expert in the family.

Pat and Marjorie Lisi at Lost Creek, Bayfield County